T[illegible]f th[illegible]y Dale Pies

by

Chris Heath

Published 1998 by
J R Nicholls, Denby Dale.

First published in 1998 by
J R Nicholls
347b Wakefield Road
Denby Dale
Huddersfield
HD8 8RT

ISBN 0 9532568 0 4

Typeset in Times New Roman

Printed & bound in Great Britain by
E. M. Walker & Son Ltd, Clayton West

Front cover illustration: Pie Day celebrations 1928, photographed from the viaduct over Wakefield Road.
Courtesy of Leach Lithoprint, Brighouse.

Dedication

For my Mum, with love,
and without whom.....

Acknowledgements

Grateful thanks must be given to the following, without whose earlier research and assistance this book may never have come to print:

John Rumsby, Tolson Museum, Huddersfield.
Nora Kitson and John Netherwood, fellow 'Pie' chroniclers.
The Sheffield Telegraph.
The Huddersfield Examiner.
Leach Lithoprint, Brighouse.
BBC Radio Leeds.
David Bostwick - Pie Historian and author of 'An Illustrated Narrative History' of the Denby Dale Pies.

Contents

PART ONE

The History of the Denby Dale Pies

The village of Denby Dale has ancient links to the arts of pie making. The first of its giant pies was reputedly baked in 1788, though it is perfectly feasible that there were others prior to this. Whether earlier ones were cooked to celebrate a national or international event, or were simply the results of a good harvest safely gathered, will probably never be known. Today, the baking of monster pies in the village has a national reputation - a unique claim to fame - hence the boasts made by the signposts as one enters the village.

Since the industrial revolution Denby Dale has grown as a village, and its population multiplied into the bustling and thriving community we have today. Initially known as Denby Dykeside, its early history is identical to that of its near neighbours, Upper and Lower Denby, sited in the hills above the valley of the River Dearne. Indeed, the river itself provided power for corn mills, and later factories, which caused the beginnings of the settlement we know today. Isolated farmsteads, cottages at Haywood Bottom, Wood Nook and others, would have been scattered amongst the hills in the Dale below Denby, running alongside the course of the Dyke known as the Dearne, in the years prior to the eighteenth century.

It was also at Haywood Bottom where the ‘cucking stool’ or ‘ducking stool’, the tried and trusted way of finding out a witch, was sited. Evidence for this remains in the name ‘Cuckstool’ Road, which was later built rising up out of the valley above Haywood.

People living in this valley were included within the Township of Denby in major tax records, such as the Hearth Tax of 1672. Prior to this they would have been under the jurisdiction of the Lords of the Manor, the Burdet family, who had held the lordship since at least the beginning of the fourteenth century. The name Denby Dyke (Side) continued to be used until the first quarter of the nineteenth century when its isolation decreased with the coming of two turnpike roads, the textile industry and, a little later, the railway.

For many years the wooden bridge that spanned the Dearne by the corn mill at the bottom of Miller Hill had served as an important crossing point for traders and travellers. Used daily by packhorses, its subsequent demise due to floods in 1706 caused merchants to seek alternative and longer routes. The sum of £7 10s was paid to the Lord of Gunthwaite, Godfrey Bosville, to begin work on a replacement bridge; but a further £40 was required to complete the work, the amount being raised by the villagers themselves. Corn Mills were in operation before and during the eighteenth century along the course of the Dearne, the one at the bottom of Miller Hill as we have seen, and others, notably owned by the Shirt family of Jowitt House, Dakinbrook.

Wakefield Road, Denby Dale during the procession of the 1928 Pie.
Courtesy of Leach Lithoprint, Brighouse.

The Return To Sanity of George III - Pie Number One

Every so often, the quiet, sleepy village of Denby Dale loses its anonymity and achieves world-wide attention. Every generation or so an enormous pie is baked, the traditions of which began over two hundred years ago.

The first mention of a pie in the village is recorded in 1788, though this date seems to be slightly spurious. The reason is the event for which the pie was baked, the return to sanity of King George III. George, who had come to the throne of England in 1760, suffered a serious illness in 1765 and showed symptoms which were later linked to his 'madness' of 1788. This 'madness' caused the King to foam at the mouth, talk incessantly for twenty four hours at a time, scream sexual and other obscenities and even engage in conversation with an oak tree which he believed to be Frederick of Prussia. To combat this madness the King was moved from Windsor to Kew in December, where, by modern standards he was horrendously treated. His mouth was gagged, burning poultices were applied to his body to drive away evil and he was strapped to a chair for hours.

His 'madness', which later opinion has suggested was porphyria, a rare metabolic disease which can poison the nervous system and, in extreme cases the brain, passed, and in April 1789 a service of thanksgiving was held at St. Pauls Cathedral to celebrate his recovery.

This would seem to suggest that either the villagers of Denby Dyke were pre-empting the future or that the pie was actually baked in 1789. The only claim for a 1788 pie would seem to rest with the build up of the Kings illness in that year where, after suffering a 'bilious attack', he retired to Cheltenham to partake of the spa waters. It seems possible that news of an improvement in the Kings condition could have reached Denby Dyke and that their elation caused them to bake a pie.

Leaving aside the year, very little is known about the beginning of this 200-year-old tradition. It would appear that a large game pie was cooked at the White Hart Inn (now Mr Boon's) and was served to the villagers in Cliffe Style field behind the Memorial Hall which was demolished in the late 1970's. The foundation for the baking of a large pie to celebrate local or national events was now firmly in place and, if one takes the date 1788 as the beginning, then it was another 27 years before another entered the annals of history.

King George III

The Victory Pie - Pie Number Two (1815)

In the early nineteenth century, fears of a French invasion were paramount in the thoughts of England's population. Napoleon Boneparte, by virtue of his conquests in Europe, was threatening to march his armies across the Channel and do what only William the Conqueror had managed to do; subdue and conquer England. It was no small sigh of relief that the country breathed when the Duke of Wellington defeated 'Boney' at Waterloo in 1815, thereby freeing the country from threat of invasion and establishing peace. The country rejoiced and the people of Denby Dale baked another pie to celebrate.

The pie, by today's standards was comparatively small; containing twenty fowls, two sheep and half a peck of flour for the crust. It was baked in an oven at the old Corn Mill, next to the Dearne at the bottom of Miller Hill.

In his book, 'The Denby Dale Pies', David Bostwick commented on the Waterloo veteran, George Wilby, who hung his sword over the drawing room mantelpiece at his home, Pogstone House, Cuckstool, Denby Dale. Mr Bostwick notes that the triumphant return of this man could only have given impetus to the baking of this 'Victory' pie and that he may well have had the honour of carving the pie with his sword. It may also be that he set the precedent for subsequent ceremonial carvings, for a specially commissioned knife and fork were used for the next pie, the knife being cut to the shape of a sabre.

The Repeal of the Corn Laws - Pie Number Three

(29 August 1846)

As a result of the end of the Napoleonic wars an act was brought forward in 1815 by Liverpool's Robert Jenkinson to protect landed interest following the collapse of artificially high prices of corn and other cereals. During the wars British farmers had been encouraged to grow as much domestic produce as possible as imports from the continent were negligible. Now the wars were over, these British farmers feared that imports from Europe would substantially reduce the price and therefore ruin them. This new act was an attempt to protect them until the price of British corn was 80s a quarter; this was fine for the farmers but not so good for the poor. The result of the act was to keep the price of bread high, when bread was the staple diet of the poor.

The act became the symbol of the repression of the poor and found a unique voice in that of Ebenezer Elliott (1781-1849). From Rotherham in South Yorkshire, Elliott, who became known as the 'Corn Law Rhymer' wrote:

> *'Whoever does not oppose the Corn Law is a patron of want, national immorality, bankruptcy, child-murder, incendiary fires, midnight assassination and anarchy'.*

He became nationally established as a social critic in 1831 after the publication of his 'Corn Law Rhymes', which attacked the 'Bread Tax'. He was a supporter of the Anti Corn Law League, headed by the Liberal MP's Cobden and Bright and yet, for all the political agitation he and they caused, the act was not repealed until 1846 by Peel's outgoing government. Thirty-one years of hardship for the poorer classes had ended and Denby Dale celebrated by baking their third recorded pie.

This pie was probably the most important in community terms, actually celebrating something which directly and adversely affected them. It was also the first real 'monster' pie. A village poet recorded the event in rhyme:

Come all ye lads of Denby Dale
And listen to me awhile;
A tale so true I'll tell to you
'Twill cause you all to smile.
In 1846 they resolved to have a meal
And drink the health of three great men,
Cobden, Bright and Peel.

They made a thumping pie my boys,
Such a one you never saw;
It took eight horses large and strong
From the oven it to draw.

You poachers of the countryside
May each lay down his gun,
For pheasants, partridges and ground game,
We've killed them every one.

The rabbits too will have to rue,
For if they show a tail,
They'll all be shot and in the pot
Be eat at Denby Dale.

The pigeons, too, will all get killed
If they don't quickly fly;
For they must also do their share
In filling this great pie.

At Clayton West they did their best;
A pudding they had made.
But Denby Dale made them turn pale
When rejoicing at Free Trade.

Cobden

Bright

Peel

Ebenezer Elliott would not have been oblivious to the event as his sister Mary had married the Waterloo veteran George Wilby and it would appear that the pie was baked close to where the couple lived.

David Bostwick noted that oral tradition remembered a building, in front of Cuckstool farmhouse which served as a dye house and plasterers workshop, which was used to house the oven and bake the 1846 pie. A circular iron dish, 7 feet 10 inches in diameter and 22 inches deep was used to contain the following, mind-boggling list of ingredients:

> *$44^{1}/_{2}$ stones of flour, 19lbs of lard, 16lbs of butter, 7 hares, 14 rabbits, 4 pheasants, 4 grouse, 2 ducks, 2 geese, 2 turkeys, 2 guinea fowls, 4 hens, 6 pigeons, 63 small birds, 5 sheep, 1 calf and 100lbs of beef.*

The pie-dish was lined with pastry into which the whole of the above were placed and covered with a pastry top. After $10^{1}/_{2}$ hours of baking it was removed from the oven and put onto a dray to be towed from Cuckstool to Norman Park, to the accompaniment of three bands.

Finally, the procession complete, the pie was put onto a temporary platform in front of a fast-growing crowd of people. The attending dignitaries made speeches as the stage began to fill up with more and more people. Inevitably, the weight on the stage became too much and it gave way. An estimated crowd of

15,000 people surged forward and during the following state of riot and turmoil the stage was demolished and the pie destroyed. Many people managed to collect pieces of its crust and even waded into the dish so as to be able to partake of the pie; but the occasion was effectively ruined.

Another version of the disastrous day's proceedings suggests that it was a Tory plot to ruin the largely Liberal celebrations and that certain men were bribed to vandalise the platform. That it was a politically motivated act of sabotage seems to gain in authenticity when one considers a letter written by a Mr Jonas France of Middlesborough, who disclosed the truth to the Huddersfield Examiner some years later:

> *'I think that you will get information about the pie coming to grief before it got served out through the Tories getting all the navvies they could together and walking them about half drunk. At a given signal they were to rush at the wagon the pie was on and trample it to pieces, which they did'.*

Mr Joseph Peace, who should have had the honour of cutting the pie, was denied that right. According to tradition he made such a lengthy speech that two men from Clayton West grew bored and knocked out some of the platform supports; the stage collapsed and Mr Peace fell into the pie.

This could also have been an act of sabotage. Clayton West had already made a 16 stone plum pudding to celebrate the Act's repeal, and perhaps did not relish the thought of being outdone by their near neighbours.

It is clear that there were numerous stories concerning the abrupt termination of the days proceedings, probably emanating from the confusion caused in the ensuing riot. Whether people from Clayton West were involved or not, they certainly had their noses in front of the Denby Daler's that year.

The Golden Jubilee Pie - Pie Numbers Four and Five

(27 August 1887 & 3 September 1887)

Queen Victoria's Golden Jubilee finally caused the people of Denby Dale to risk baking a fourth giant pie. Forty-one years had passed since the fiasco of 1846 and a new generation had yet to experience such an occasion, but there must have been a few nerves jangling as the decision was taken.

The village itself had changed enormously in the intervening years. The railway had come, being constructed since 1845. The first viaduct, a wooden one built in 1846, was damaged by a storm in the winter of 1847 whilst still under construction, but the line finally opened on 1 July 1850. A stone viaduct, which was officially opened in 1880, eventually replaced the wooden one.

Travel and trade opportunities opened up new worlds to the villagers and the industries that had settled in the valley. Home-based handloom weaving had gradually given way as mechanisation took over and mills began to tempt a ready supply of skilled workers into their factories. Three major ones sprang up in Denby Dale, Z. Hinchliffe & Sons in 1850, Jonas Kenyon & Sons in 1854 and Brownhill and Scatchard in 1868, all identifying a skilled and available labour source alongside the power to be derived from the River Dearne. The Naylor's and Joe Kitson's groups began manufacturing earthenware pipes and bricks as the opportunities to reach more distant markets opened up. Indeed Naylor's grew in Denby Dale after being given the contract to build the stone viaduct in 1877.

New housing was needed to supply the large influx of people moving to the village seeking work as the demand increased and the size of the village and its population grew accordingly.

A Committee was formed to oversee affairs and it was decided that this pie should be larger than any before and that the funds for it should be raised by public subscription. It was also decided that the people of Denby Dale, children and the old aged should get a share first, before allowing the general public its opportunity.

The Committee designed fund-raising ventures that would hopefully cover the cost of staging the event and, with luck, leave a little over to be used for local charities. Sixpence each was to be charged for viewing the pie. A funfair and refreshments were organised and plates were commissioned for sale, these bearing a portrait of Queen Victoria and the relevant dates and sizes relating to the day. Special train services were run from Bradford, Dewsbury and Halifax. The simple village feast had now moved on a stage and was expected to pull in crowds from much further afield.

For the first time the Pie was to remain in a dish, thereby dispelling fears of any possible repetition of the 1846 proceedings. Prior to this the Pies had been 'stand pies', similar in looks to huge pork pies, with only the pastry sides and crust holding it together.

W.C. Holmes & Co. of Huddersfield, notable for making gasometers, were given the contract to construct the dish. At 15cwts, it was 8 feet in diameter and 2 feet deep and made from riveted sheet steel and angle iron; it was the biggest so far. A special oven was designed by J. Drake and Sons of Halifax, and built behind the White Hart Inn. It consisted of 3,000 red bricks, 5,000 firebricks, 50 enamelled bricks and 30cwts of fireclay, all of which were supplied by Kitson's Brick and Tile Company of Denby Dale. This huge oven, which was 14 feet square on the outside and 10 feet square on the inside, was flued so as to equalise the heat in all parts of the pie. A stewing boiler adjoined the oven, made by Mr Joseph Barraclough the Blacksmith on Smithy Hill in Upper Denby. Holding 80 gallons, the meat was stewed before being placed in the pie.

A firm of professional bakers from Halifax was to supervise the baking. The pie Committee employed F. Workman & Sons for this unenviable task, and even though they were professional bakers they would never have overseen anything like this before! The ingredients alone should have been enough to put them off:

> *1,581lbs. of beef, 163lbs. of veal, 180lbs of lamb, 180lbs of mutton, 250lbs of lean pork, 40 pigeons, 42 fowls, 3 hares, 64 rabbits, 12 grouse, 21 ducks, 4 plovers, 1 turkey, 5 geese, 2 wild ducks, 108 small birds, 20lbs of suet and 42 stones of potatoes.*

The professional bakers hired a London chef for the project, though on the night before the big day this man caught a train back to the capital; it was a warning.

A large amount of the meat to be used in the pie had been exhibited in the village butchers shop - remember to consider that it was the middle of summer. This was then cut up and cooked in the boiler in batches before being transferred to the pie dish. Freshly cooked hot meat and gravy was then added to that which had already been deposited in the dish, lying there going cold. Placed in layers around the inside edge of the dish were game birds, which were meant to cook when the pie finally entered the oven. To fill the dish, the 42 stones of potatoes were added, the whole lying under earthenware bowls of gravy helping to support the crust that was placed over a layer of canvas. With its crust and including the dish the pie weighed nearly $1^1/_2$ tons.

Just before midnight on Thursday 25th August the pie entered the oven to be cooked. It remained there until 10 o'clock on Friday, when it was removed and placed in an outhouse to cool before the big day.

Although the pie was reported to be done to a turn, Mr Workman also left the village on Friday night never to be seen again. Either he and the London chef left together or the two have become confused with one another. Either way, they knew what the Committee, the villagers and the tourists would find out the following day.

Many thousands of people swarmed into the village intent on having a good time and of course a piece of the giant pie. The programme of the day's events promised that the pie would be on view from 1.00pm to 3.30pm in Norman Park and that when the locals, children and the old had been served, the general public were to have their share. However, those without a programme would have been unaware of these arrangements, as they were never publicly announced.

The pie was placed onto a wagon and was ready to begin its ceremonial procession around the village by 11.30am on the Saturday morning. It left the White Hart (now Mr Boon's) bedecked with flowers, and was drawn by nine horses taking it to its destination at Norman Park where a large tent had been erected, fitted with seats and tables. This was the viewing point for the public.

Crowds of people had flocked to the village causing crushes around the barriers circling the marquee, so much so that the procession of 700 schoolchildren, led by Denby Dale Brass Band, struggled to reach the enclosure as people held on to their vantage points with grim determination. People were already beginning to sneak into the tent and the flower trimmings on the pie were hastily grabbed whilst the carvers took their positions, waiting for the 3.30pm deadline for cutting the pie.

The Chairman of the Committee, Mr H.J. Brierley, had been given this honour, but no sooner had he stood to make his speech than the crowd surged forward clamouring for a piece of the pie. This tactic proved effective and, as the police stood around helpless, people were trying to break off pieces of crust. Another fiasco in the making was about to take a turn for the worse. Amidst the confusion, ceremony was abandoned and the knife was sliced into the pie. Like the parting of the Red Sea the uncontrollable crowd suddenly melted back and away as the most nauseating stench began to fill the atmosphere. The twenty-foot berth given to the offending object would seem to have implied that the pie was somewhat 'gamey'. To a bystander the comic about-turn by the once eager people, for whom by now just a sniff of the pie was enough, must have been mellowed by the thoughts of the officials and the police in as much as serious injury had probably been avoided.

The arranged programme of events could not now be carried out, as people ventured forth still trying to grab pieces of crust and any other items that were fit to eat. Finally Mr Brierley announced that when the old folk had been served (presumably if they still wanted to be served) the pie would be taken into the open field and distributed accordingly.

The once majestic record breaker now sat in melancholy embarrassment, its crust ripped to shreds and its trimmings gone. The crowds had begun to melt away and the day was effectively over, and ruined. The accounts told a sorry tale:

Hire of marquee and small tent	*£ 19 17s 6d*
Damage to same	*£ 14 3s 1½ d*

Evidently the cooking procedure had been at fault, and reports of a brace of gamey grouse and what looked to be a skinned fox can't have helped matters. The crowds must have suffered mixed emotions, probably ranging from hilarity and bewilderment to a sense of feeling cheated.

The remains of the pie made a final journey on Sunday 28th August. A funeral procession sombrely made its way up to Toby Wood where the contents of the dish were emptied into a pit and buried in quicklime. Perhaps somewhat ridiculously a funeral card was printed, as was the tradition at the time when a loved one had passed away.

'In Affectionate Remembrance of the Denby Dale Pie, which died August 27th 1887, aged three days'.

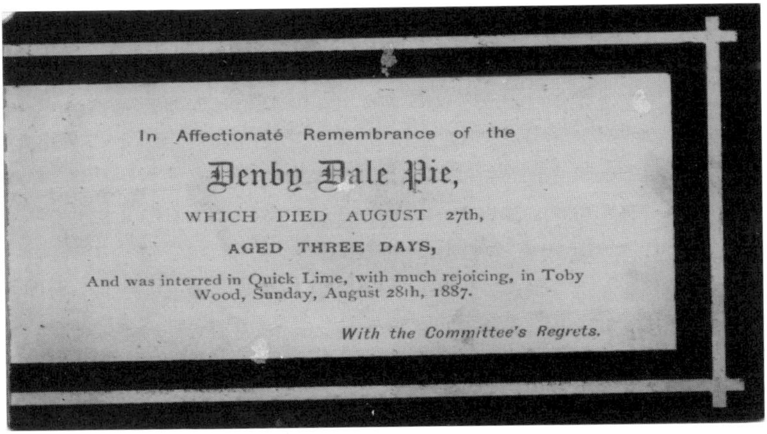

In Affectionaté Remembrance of the

Denby Dale Pie,

WHICH DIED AUGUST 27th,

AGED THREE DAYS,

And was interred in Quick Lime, with much rejoicing, in Toby Wood, Sunday, August 28th, 1887.

With the Committee's Regrets.

The memorial card for the 1887 pie.

The verse read as follows:

Strong was the smell that compelled us to part,
From a treat to our stomach and a salve to our heart;
Like the last Denby Dale Pie which the crowd did ssail,
Its contents a rank mixture, it quickly turned stale;
Though we could not eat, yet we still lingered near,
Till the stench proved too much for a nassals to bear;
So like sensible men the committee did say:
'Twas better to inter it without further delay.

The card seems to have been distributed to the villagers the following weekend as a note at the bottom says:

'Undeterred by previous efforts the people of Denby Dale have attempted another pie, which is to be consumed today, Saturday. This has been made by the ladies of the village, and is expected to be a success. It consists of 48 stones of flour, 96 stones of potatoes, a heifer, 2 calves and 2 sheep'.

The Committee gave the following explanation:

'The fifth pie was prepared for September 3, 1887 by the Committee of the fourth pie who felt it their duty to provide the inhabitants of the District, who were prevented by the crush, from partaking of the previous pie'.

This time there was no publicity, no professional baker and..... No Game! Indeed game was never used again in a Denby Dale Pie.

All the animals were slaughtered on the preceding Thursday and were cooked on the Friday. The ladies of the village made the pastry in the small hours of Saturday morning; indeed they made two crusts. An inner crust which covered the meat and an outer one which rested on skewers and chicken wire. Once baked, the pie was placed on a stone-cart to be drawn by two horses to Inkerman Mills where it would be distributed.

Inside the mill, the adults were served in one room, the children in another. The older residents received a gill of beer and along with the children were given a piece of pie to take home. The Committee members atoned well for the previous week's fiasco.

As with the previous pie a Commemorative Plate was issued, this time showing two portraits of Queen Victoria, one from the beginning of her reign and the other as she was at the time of the pie. The sale of the plates substantially aided the costs of both ventures and, when the accounts were drawn up, it was found that a profit of £119 14s 9½d had been made. This was distributed to local charities.

The Corn Laws Jubilee Pie - Pie Number Six (1st August 1896)

After an almost hasty gap of only 9 years, the Denby Dalers were at it again! Contemporary writers seem to struggle with the reasons for this. Considering the problems that beset the previous two offerings, one would have thought the villagers would have wanted to wait a full generation before being subjected to similar events again. Undaunted however, the fiftieth anniversary of the repeal of the hated Corn Laws was a good enough occasion to warrant such excess again. It is likely that feelings still ran high and that only with the passing of time have we forgotten the deprivation caused by the lack of food to the poorer classes.

The villagers had certainly not forgotten their hardships and one man in particular was chosen for the singular honour of leading the procession on the day. Mr Joseph Hirst, by now 88 years old, had taken part in the original struggle to have the laws lifted; he had also been present at the 1846 pie. He travelled in a cart drawn by two grey horses flanked alongside by his two grandsons whose mode of dress represented the expensive loaf during the Act's imposition and the cheap loaf after its repeal. David Bostwick recorded that:

> *"One in rags and tatters carried a banner bearing the words 'Corn 4 shillings a stone, 1846' and the other one dressed in good West Riding cloth held a placard with the words 'Corn 1 shilling a stone, 1896'".*

A feature in the Huddersfield Examiner dated June 7th 1988 concerned the longevity of my own ancestor Mr Douglas Heath, the former blacksmith in Denby Dale. He was 95 when he was interviewed and was only $3^1/_2$ when the pie was made, but he still had a mental picture of the parade and remembered being carried up on horseback into the park where the festivities took place. He also remembered the two grandsons of Mr Hirst, recalling:

'There were two lads, one with a real smart suit and the other one all in rags. I think they were Ned Lockwood and Edwin Hirst'.

The lessons of the past had been learned and were duly observed by the Committee who kept faith with local ability in preparing and cooking the pie. Five local experts were to supervise a team of local ladies and the dish used in 1887 was to be scrubbed clean and used again. The experts were W. Spivey and Fred Dearnley and the women, J. Parker, Mrs. Charles Wood of Denby Dale and Mrs. Stafford of Ingbirchworth. The gross weight of dish with its contents was 35cwts.

The following list of contents now omits all game and poultry:

1,120lb of beef, 180lbs veal, 112lbs mutton, 60lbs lamb, 1,120lbs flour and 160lbs lard.

The dish used for the 1887 and 1896 Pies (from a picture to promote the 1928 pie). Courtesy of Leach Lithoprint, Brighouse.

The cooks of the 1896 pie, together with the pie itself.
Courtesy of Leach Lithoprint, Brighouse.

It took 6 hours to cook the meat and 2 1/2 hours to bake the crust in an oven measuring 9ft wide, 14ft long and 2ft high. Allot Brothers of Denby Dale built it behind Mr Horn's Corn Mill in the village.

The Committee was expecting large crowds of people to turn up, indeed estimates for anywhere between 60,000 and 100,000 people proved to be correct. Again lessons had been learned and the wooden platform in Norman Park, where the pie was to be cut was solidly built and surrounded with barricading. Further barriers were erected in the field to stop the crowd rushing the platform as the pie was cut; the platform was draped with an awning and bedecked with floral trimmings.

The programme of events for the day was listed in the programme thus:

10.00 am	The Pie leaves the oven for Norman Park, drawn by 14 horses.
11.00 - 4.00	The Pie will be on view in the Park.
3.00	Procession of Band, waiters etc. from the White Hart Inn.
4.00	Presentation of carvers by Mr W. Wood to Mr Frank Naylor who will then cut into the Pie.
4.30	Serving of the Pie to the general public.

The Pie was covered by a white cloth and decked with flowers aboard its wagon whilst the procession took place. The programme reported that the carvers;

'...are of a very elegant design, with buck horn handles and silver mountings, having been supplied by Mr William Lockwood, Jeweller etc. of Victoria Lane, Huddersfield. The knife is 33 inches long (with an inscription on the blade) and the fork 25 inches long'.

By 4.30pm the Medical Officer of Health in charge (Mr Alistair McGregor) had certified the pie fit to eat and the public finally got its chance. A shilling bought a helping of pie and another shilling bought a Souvenir Plate. The twelve servers issued around 2,000 portions.

The day's festivities continued during and after the serving, the Denby Dale Brass Band played throughout the afternoon, a Variety Company played, incorporating 9 different acts, and a 'Grand Display of Fireworks' rounded off what had turned out to be a very successful day. The organisers could breathe a sigh of relief; they had buried the memories of nine years ago, and after all the expenses had been paid local charities benefited.

The 1896 pie.

The Infirmary Pie - Pie Number Seven (28th August 1928).

It took the Denby Dalers a long time to decide to bake another pie. Thirty-two years had passed since the success of last time and a new generation had never experienced this most singular of village traditions. Austerity caused by the First World War had rendered possibilities of celebrating its end impractical and any ideas were soon abandoned - though some of the older residents regarded this later date as a delayed celebration. However, the fact that Huddersfield Royal Infirmary required funds urgently to improve its services was the major factor in the decision to venture forth and bake again.

Before the inauguration of the National Health Service, hospitals depended very much on voluntary contributions, indeed almost every Church and Chapel in the country had an 'Infirmary Sunday', where the collection was used solely for the benefit of the local hospital. At a public meeting it was decided that a belated 'Victory Pie' would best show the village's appreciation for the work of the hospital and to this end work began. £1,000 was needed to endow a cot in the hospital, to be known as the 'Denby & Cumberworth Cot'.

The whole village became involved with the preparations, every house was decorated with a view to get the village looking its best for the estimated 60,000 visitors expected, and the local newspapers began to report on the tales coming from the village.

Tickets for the field were being sold in London, Newcastle, Hull, Birmingham and many other major cities and special trains and coaches were being laid on.

The Public Houses in the village requested extended opening hours. Ernest Moorhouse of the Prospect Hotel (now The Dalesman) and J H Lockwood of the Foresters Inn, Lower Cumberworth, requested that they be allowed to open from 10am to 3pm and from 5.30pm to 10.30pm. Both requests were granted.

Constructing the oven for the 1928 pie.
Courtesy of Leach Lithoprint, Brighouse.

Because this was going to be the biggest pie to date, the old dish was now redundant and a new one was built measuring 16ft long, 5ft wide and 15 inches deep. Weighing 1 ton 15cwts, it was given by Mr G. W. Naylor, Brick and Tile Works, Denby Dale.

The Denby Dale Concrete Manufacturing Co built an oven at the Corn Mill in the village, Ruth Whitwam remembering that the labourers were:

> *Edwin Allot, Joe Noble, Albert Brown, John Hirst, Harry Bedford, Walker Williamson, Arthur Smith, Norman Whiteley, James Ronald Whitwam and Wright Beaumont.*

This time the ingredients were:

> *4 bullocks, 600lb of beef, 15cwts potatoes, 80 stones flour, 2 cwts lard and 2 stones of baking powder.*

This meant that there was 100 cubic feet of pie, which was enough for 20,000 people to have nearly 1/4 of a pound each.

Five local butchers, Mr W. A. Heap, Mr G.T.M. Lea, Mr Norman Naylor, Mr Tom Schofield, Mr George Senior, who had the help of Mr William Wood (Chairman of both 1887 pies), aided 18 local women chosen as cooks who included:

> *Mrs Crossland, Mrs Firth, Mrs Barrowclough, Mrs Cunningham, Mrs Littlewood, Mrs Stanger, Mrs Mosley, Mrs Lockwood, Mrs Senior, Mrs Wood, and Mrs Cooper, who were led by Mrs Jonas Kenyon (of Kenyons Textile Manufacturers on Dearnside).*

The beef for the pie was cooked in the Ambulance Hall, next to the oven. The pastry had been rolled into small portions in the Salvation Army building, the dish being constructed in squares to enable the pie to be covered with pastry that didn't sink. Fat cakes were also made so that every one could have some crust to go with their pie.

Making the crust for the 1928 pie.
Courtesy of Leach Lithoprint, Brighouse.

On the Wednesday night a rehearsal was undertaken and, though initially problems occurred whilst trying to remove the dish from the oven due to the confined space, hundreds of people lined the route to be taken and the band played amidst the bunting and decoration - it was carnival time early!

On the night of Thursday, August 26th, the dish was filled with its pre-cooked delicacies, (indeed it had taken a week to complete cooking the meat!), David Bostwick noted that:

> *'A local man, Joseph Kaye, wheeled away six barrow loads of what would have been bad pie that night. Nothing was said to the Public Health Inspector. Nor was he told that the Pie dish leaked, and that to stop the gravy trickling away a poultice made of oatmeal and other things was stuffed into the dish to plug the gap'.*

The monstrous dish was mounted on wheels to enable the cooks to wheel it in and out of the fire to observe the baking process. The thirty hours baking ticked away, there was little sleep and the pie itself was guarded to prevent the unforeseen. The 'Huddersfield Examiner' noted that:

> *'Odorous whiffs were borne on a light breeze throughout the village'.*

Finally, at 1pm on Saturday the 28th, it was adjudged to be 'well done' and then the first official problem occurred; it was stuck in the oven! The wagon was waiting, the procession was due to begin at 2.15pm, what to do?

> *'T' pies bigger than thou thawt', called a witty, but concerned observer!*

A winch and hawser had done the early work but now it became expedient for men armed with crowbars to begin to try

The pie gets stuck!

and lever the steaming hot dish away from the oven. Unfortunately, crowbars proved insufficient and so were replaced by 10 foot tram rails. Aided by jacks and using short lifts the pie was at last persuaded away from its tomb, even then only after knocking part of a wall down. One local man, when asked by a reporter what was wrong, replied, 'Too many bosses'. Only for another problem to surface!

The wagon was made of soft wood; by the time the pie was only half way on it was sinking into the platform. Willing volunteers were required to place steel rails underneath before the job was done. It was now 3.15pm! The Huddersfield Examiner records:

> *'It was 3.30pm before the pie was got into position, and a mighty shout arose from the crowd gathered around the oven, which was quickly echoed by the crowds lining the route'.*

At last! The pie loaded safely onto the processional wagon.
Courtesy of Leach Lithoprint, Brighouse.

The half-mile long procession consisting of mounted police, Denby Dale Band, the ‘Pie’, bakers, cooks, floats, other decorated vehicles and people in fancy dress or representing Groups. It went through the village by way of Catch Bar to Upper Cumberworth and back to Denby Dale via Kaye Line to its destination in Norman Park to massive cheering from the patient and anxiously waiting public. Forty or fifty police were on duty to keep order but, despite the delay, great good humour had prevailed.

The pie on the wagon (finally) and in the procession to the pie field.

The procession making its way along the Barnsley Road.

Just before reaching Norman Park, as the band was playing 'On Ilkla' Moor Baht 'At', there was another little mishap. The decorated superstructure of the wagon carrying the pie got caught in the foliage of the overhanging trees and was badly crumpled, giving it a slightly shoddy appearance on arrival in the park.

Mr William Wood making the First Cut in the 1928 pie.

From the Huddersfield Examiner:
'We have delivered the goods, declared the Chairman (Mr. W. A. Heap) of the Pie Committee'.
'Not before time awther!', was the bawled comment from a vociferous and apparently voracious member of the crowd - a crowd numbering at least 40,000.

Mr William Wood had been appointed to the task of cutting the pie, a task he was well suited for due to his associations with previous pies. He used a knife of about a yard long and the fork used at the 1896 ceremony. It had not been possible to make a fork in time for Saturday though it was subsequently planned to make a matching one with a suitable inscription to Mr Wood.

In his speech he spoke of the pride, inherent in Denby Dale, in its reputation for making monster pies, and that a 'tin pot' carnival was not good enough...

The army of servers hard at work.
Courtesy of Leach Lithoprint, Brighouse.

'Ger into that pie!' the famished interrupter chimed in again at which the crowd broke into laughter. The hint was taken and the servers sprang into action.

An army of servers was needed to distribute the pie:

16 to ladle from large bowls to soup plates.
32 to carry bowls and dishes to lorries.
24 to carry full bowls from lorries to pie tables.
40 to apportion pie crust on plates.
16 to carry crust plates to pie tables.
60 to apportion and distribute the pie.
20 to carry full plates to pie tables.
12 boys to carry empty plates.
36 to deal with tickets.

Brawny butchers dug into the pie with long handled ladles once the crust was removed. They transferred the food into baths, which were in turn emptied into smaller containers and then carried to the tables to be put onto the pie plates and eaten. Everyone had either a piece of crust or a fat cake to go with it. And all for a shilling a head!

Long queues kept the servers very busy, but finally the dish was emptied and taken back to the oven where, for a small fee, people were allowed to wind it in and out of the oven, demonstrating the mechanisms simplicity!

Prizes were awarded for various categories in the parade e. g. best decorated wagon, motor wagon, cycle, motor cycle etc. Indeed my own Great Uncle, Joe Willie Heath, converted his Morgan 3 wheeler into a dummy aeroplane, though he did have to drive down from Upper Denby using the whole of the road!

The day had been, eventually, a great success. It was estimated that between 12.00 and 3.00 o'clock on Saturday between 6,000 and 7,000 people had arrived at Denby Dale station; the bookings from Huddersfield alone totalled 4,016.

The following Financial Statement makes for interesting reading and shows the grand sum of £1,147.3s.5d. raised for distribution from the day's proceedings. Huddersfield Royal Infirmary got their cot, situated in the Green Lea Nursing Home which was an annexe to the hospital, and many other local institutions benefited.

Denby Dale and District Pie and Carnival Effort, 4th August 1928.

FINANCIAL STATEMENT.

INCOME.	£ s. d.	£ s. d.
To Private Subscriptions	141 18 0	
,, Street and House Collections ...	305 16 2	
,, Street Organ Collections... ...	12 3 5	
		459 17 7
,, Plates and Tickets	1303 16 7	
,, Utensils and Goods Sold... ...	56 11 9	
,, Refreshments by Ladies	121 15 3	
,, Rock Sold	29 14 0	
		1511 17 7
,, Poetry and Songs	...	19 5 9
,, Parking of Cars and Stall Charges ...	...	56 6 4
,, Naylors Fund for Sundries ...	...	3 19 0
,, Sundries (General)	...	5 0 11
,, Bank Interest	...	1 16 0
		£2058 3 2

EXPENDITURE.	£ s. d.	£ s. d.
By Gross Cost of Oven and Dish ...		113 15 2
,, Contents of Pie	151 17 3	
,, Less Subscribed by Butchers ...	30 0 0	
		121 17 3
,, Plates Purchased		387 19 0
,, Rock		18 12 3
,, School Rent and Park Field Insurance... ...		10 2 0
,, Utensils		97 3 11
,, Procession and Decorations		15 14 8
,, Park Field and Entertainments		59 19 0
,, Printing, Stationery, Postages, etc.		82 2 6
,, Bank Charges (Cheques drawn)		9 0
,, Infirmary Bed (Endowment Plate)		3 5 0
		£910 19 9
Net Balance for Distribution £1147-3-5 as follows—		
Huddersfield Royal Infirmary ...	1050 0 0	
do. do. do. ...	12 3 5	
Denby Dale Church of England ...	6 0 0	
,, ,, Wesleyan Church ...	6 0 0	
,, ,, Primitive Church ...	6 0 0	
,, ,, Wes. Reform Church ...	6 0 0	
,, ,, Salvation Army ...	6 0 0	
District St. John Ambulance ...	6 0 0	
,, Nursing Association ...	6 0 0	
Denby Dale Band	5 10 0	
,, ,, Bowling Club ...	5 10 0	
,, ,, Cricket Club ...	5 10 0	
District British Legion	5 10 0	
Cumberworth Church of England ...	3 0 0	
,, Reform Church ...	3 0 0	
,, Primitive Church ...	3 0 0	
,, Cricket Club ...	3 0 0	
Denby Church of England ...	3 0 0	
,, Band	3 0 0	
,, Cricket Club	3 0 0	
		1147 3 5
		£2058 3 2

Approved and adopted at a General Meeting of the inhabitants of Denby Dale and District, held at the Denby Dale Church Hut, 1st July, 1929.

Councillor Fred Ellis, Chairman,
Granville S. Mosley, General Secretary.

Audited and found correct,
J. E. Dale & Co,
Accountants, Bank Chambers,
Westgate, Huddersfield,

11th day of June, 1929.

Hirst Buckley, Printer, Scissett

The final accounts for the 1928 pie, showing that a sum of £1062, 3 shillings and 5 pence was donated to the Huddersfield Royal Infirmary.

DENBY DALE PIE.

AUGUST 4TH. 1928.

WE'VE heard some fine songs about Pudding,
Chips and well mangled Tripe;
Bolton Trotters all hot with their clogs on,
Bananas well bent and all ripe.
Bread and Cheese and a big Spanish Onion,
Liver and Bacon, and Fry;
So to fill up your Little Mary
Have a tuck in of Denby Dale Pie.

CHORUS.

Pie, Pie, Denby Dale Pie,
Fill yourself up till you're dry,
Keep up the sale of it,
Get some good ale with it,
If you can eat, have a try.
Don't mess about with it,
Have a day out with it,
Then you'll sing "Hi Tiddley Hi,"
Go treat the wife with it,
Shorten her life with it,
Denby Dale—Denby Dale Pie.

Rhubarb you know can stand up for itself,
Pies made of Apples are grand,
But when you've had a plateful of Denby Dale Pie,
You'll not want to dance to the Band.
A pie made of everything of the best
To beat it the world I defy,
So thanks for what we are about to receive,
Glorious Denby Dale Pie.

W. GATTY, Barnsley.

Songsheet for the 1928 pie.

The End of the 1887 & 1896 Pie Dish

The year was 1940, British forces had been evacuated from Dunkirk in June, the Luftwaffe were abroad in the night skies and the Home Guard had been formed, things were looking bleak. On Saturday, 21st September, during the 'Battle of Britain', the Denby Dalers did their bit for the War effort.

'Pie Dish for Guns, Not Butter' was the cry of the poster announcing the imminent demise of this village relic. The dish had featured in the 1928 Pie parade but since that time had found no useful home. Attempts were made by a Mrs Whitwell of Kirkburton and by a Mr T Sheppard of the Hull Municipal Museum to buy the dish. Perhaps Mr Sheppard would have been successful had his timing not clashed with the desire of the villagers to part with it to raise money for the war effort and provide scrap iron. The Pie dish was hardly a national treasure and was therefore not immune to the requirements of the time.

Mr Douglas Heath remembered that he and his father, Walter had used the dish for a time as a 'slaking' trough at their blacksmith's premises on Wakefield Road, but whether the dish was removed from there to be auctioned, or had found another home, is unknown. It is likely, however, that they possessed the dish sometime between 1896 and 1928.

A large poster was printed announcing the 'Farewell to the 1887 Pie Dish'. Under an escort of the local Civil Defence Services the dish was to be taken to the Central Salvage Dump. Its journey would take it through Lower & Upper Cumberworth, Birdsedge, High Flatts and Denby with collections being made along the way. As the poster stated:

> *'BE MORE THAN GENEROUS - our local boys serving in the forces deserve our support'.*

The procession was accompanied by the Denby Dale Silver Prize Band and fund raising events included a 'Grand Cricket Match', between Mr Thackra's and Mr Lockwood's elevens where admission was 6d. There was also a competition to guess the weight of the Pie Dish, an exhibition of Pie relics in the Council School, and Bowling, Whist Drives & Dances were held in Denby Dale, Denby and Birdsedge.

At 3.00pm in the Slade, Mr G. H. Wilby offered the dish in a series of Auctions where temporary certificates of ownership were given; this alone raised the sum (according to the balance sheet overleaf) of £89.10s.0d., the owners not keen to keep such a monstrous thing in their front rooms! A few rusted pieces of the dish were broken off and sold independently, but eventually the bulk of it was handed over to the Chairman of the Council by Mr. Frank Naylor.

The dish had been on view in Norman Croft since Tuesday the 17th of September but was now on its final journey, never to be seen again in Denby Dale.

Incidentally, the 1928 Pie Dish ended its days submerged in a field behind the railway viaduct being used as a dewpond!

The Coronation of Queen Elizabeth II in 1953 would have been an excellent opportunity for the 'Dalers' to celebrate in their own inimitable style, but as with the 1928 Pie, food restrictions were still in place. The application for the necessary meat and fat for such a monster Pie was naturally turned down. An attempt was made from an unlikely source to enable the event to go ahead. The 'Farmer's and Settler's Association', of New South Wales in Australia, offered Denby Dale 1,400lbs of beef, the idea being that the British Government would release the meat from their stocks and that the Australians would replace it. Unfortunately, time was against the opportunity; the arrangements could not be made in time for the Coronation and so the offer was turned down.

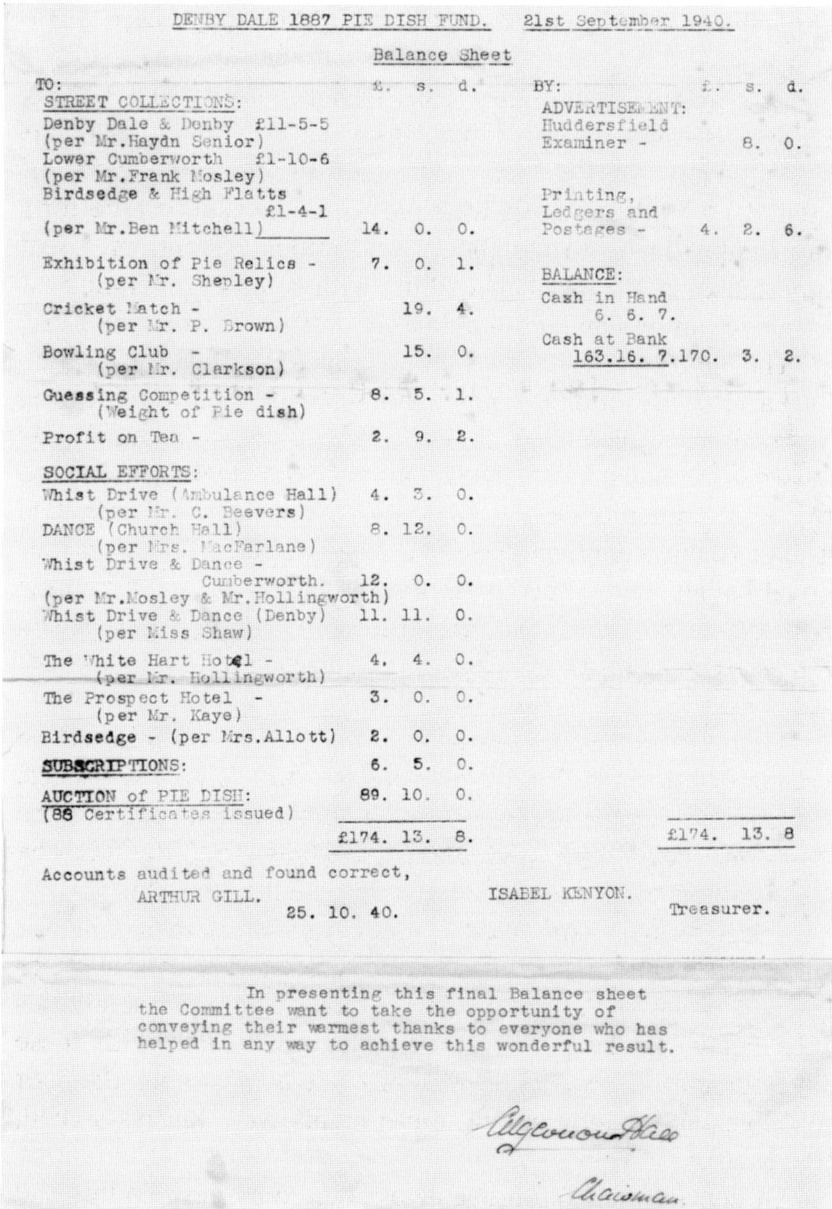

DENBY DALE 1887 PIE DISH FUND. 21st September 1940.

Balance Sheet

TO:	£.	s.	d.
STREET COLLECTIONS:			
Denby Dale & Denby £11-5-5 (per Mr.Haydn Senior)			
Lower Cumberworth £1-10-6 (per Mr.Frank Mosley)			
Birdsedge & High Flatts £1-4-1 (per Mr.Ben Mitchell)	14.	0.	0.
Exhibition of Pie Relics - (per Mr. Shepley)	7.	0.	1.
Cricket Match - (per Mr. P. Brown)		19.	4.
Bowling Club - (per Mr. Clarkson)		15.	0.
Guessing Competition - (Weight of Pie dish)	8.	5.	1.
Profit on Tea -	2.	9.	2.
SOCIAL EFFORTS:			
Whist Drive (Ambulance Hall) (per Mr. C. Beevers)	4.	3.	0.
DANCE (Church Hall) (per Mrs. MacFarlane)	8.	12.	0.
Whist Drive & Dance - Cumberworth. (per Mr.Mosley & Mr.Hollingworth)	12.	0.	0.
Whist Drive & Dance (Denby) (per Miss Shaw)	11.	11.	0.
The White Hart Hotel - (per Mr. Hollingworth)	4.	4.	0.
The Prospect Hotel - (per Mr. Kaye)	3.	0.	0.
Birdsedge - (per Mrs.Allott)	2.	0.	0.
SUBSCRIPTIONS:	6.	5.	0.
AUCTION of PIE DISH: (88 Certificates issued)	89.	10.	0.
	£174.	13.	8.

BY:	£.	s.	d.
ADVERTISEMENT: Huddersfield Examiner -		8.	0.
Printing, Ledgers and Postages -	4.	2.	6.
BALANCE:			
Cash in Hand 6. 6. 7.			
Cash at Bank 163.16. 7.	170.	3.	2.
	£174.	13.	8

Accounts audited and found correct,
ARTHUR GILL.
25. 10. 40.

ISABEL KENYON.
Treasurer.

In presenting this final Balance sheet the Committee want to take the opportunity of conveying their warmest thanks to everyone who has helped in any way to achieve this wonderful result.

Algernon Hall
Chairman

The final balance sheet of the fund raising for the disposal of the 1887 and 1897 pie dish, showing how £89 10 shillings was raised by auctioning temporary certificates of ownership of the dish.

The Village Hall Pie - Pie Number Eight (5th September 1964)

At a meeting held in the Denby Dale Memorial Hall in 1963 the decision was taken to embark on work culminating in the biggest Denby Dale Pie ever. The food rationing at the end of the Second World War, as we have seen, had scuppered efforts for Denby Dale to celebrate a National event of great importance in its usual style but, with a new generation of people to impress and, after a 36-year gap, preparations began.

The members of the meeting voted unanimously for the Pie, with a view to building a new Community Hall as its purpose. Any extra profit was to benefit the National Playing Fields Association, but many thought that baking the Pie should also be to commemorate a National event. The Committee struggled, but were then presented with the perfect answer; four Royal babies were expected in the same year for the first time in 200 years. The four were: Prince Edward, Lady Helen Windsor, Lady Sarah Armstrong Jones and James Ogilvy - how obliging of the Royal family!

The Committee took every possible step to ensure success. Veterans of the 1928 Pie were consulted and gladly gave advice, though none wished to take an active part. The rule was set; one man - one pie! Joseph Kaye proved an exception to the rule - he was a cook in 1928 and agreed to help bake the new one.

Local farmers consented to donate some of their land for the day for parking purposes and Fred and Edward Bates allowed Norman Park to be the centre of the days festivities once again. To keep the local public up to date with these developments a newsletter was produced, informing them of schedules and entertainment; these letters were always signed, 'Pie Man'.

Of course, the Committee also required money. To this end many fund raising events were organised which included: A Fashion Show, a Children's Party, A Traction Engine Rally, 2 Motor Rallies, a Bonfire and Barbecue, the sale of the usual memorabilia, Nora Kitson's excellent History of the Pies and thousands of Pie plates distributed by Alfred George.

Luckily for the Committee, a Denby Dale Pie was an excellent marketing opportunity for businesses and so the following were received with grateful thanks:

Brian Kitson's Company, Aireworth Engineering, made a dish measuring 18feet by 6feet by 18inches deep, and George Naylor of the Naylor Brothers Group in Denby Dale constructed an oven. The Electricity & Gas Boards supplied power, the Daily Mail provided the meat, Job Earnshaw & Brothers, farmers of West Cumberland, supplied the potatoes, Stafford Allen & Sons gave the spices; and so the list goes on.

Baking the Pie itself was the most important consideration of all. George Saville and his fellow butchers had the problem of creating the monster from 3 tons of beef, $1^1/_2$ tons of potatoes, $^1/_2$ ton of gravy and seasoning, $^1/_2$ ton of flour and $^1/_2$ ton of lard.

Hector Buckley's newly built milking parlour at Dry Hill was the venue for all this activity, although this meant that the gradient of Miller Hill had to be considered as this would form a part of the Pie's ceremonial processional route. Dividing the dish into sections that were individually covered with plates solved the problem. The other main problem was the Public Health Inspector. All the cooks had to have medical checks to prove their suitability and conditions in the milking parlour were kept totally sterile. Heated pokers inserted into the dish were used to maintain its temperature whilst on route to Norman Park. These stringent regulations probably caused no end of anxiety amongst the cooks but a local man, Mr Raymond Haigh of Upper Denby, did redress the balance a little.

Mr Haigh, a coalman of impressive stature, was on sentry duty at the door of the milking parlour where he refused the Public Health officials entry when they came to inspect the pie whilst it was baking. Unlike the cooks, the inspectors had not been subject to any medical and therefore were not able to prove their cleanliness!

In Raymond's own words (taken from a documentary broadcast on Radio Leeds in 1988):

'I started at teatime, Friday night, and I was in charge. I had a list of 22 names, 22 people who were allowed into the place where they were actually baking the pie; and no other person was allowed in. In those days they called this area Denby Dale Urban District Council, it wasn't under Kirklees then, and they had their own Public Health Inspector called Mr Urmstone. On Saturday morning two big, posh cars rolled up and two gentlemen got out of these cars and met Mr Urmstone who brought them to the door and introduced me to them. Both were Chief Public Health Inspectors and had come to see that things were going right.
I said, 'Oh yes, just a minute Mr Urmstone', so I got my list. I knew Mr Urmstone's name was on the list of course. I said, 'now, what are your names gentlemen?', and they told me and I said, 'well....you're not on my list, so you can't come in!'
Mr Urmstone said, 'I know Raymond, but they are Chief Public Health Inspectors'. I replied, 'Oh are they? - yes - well, THEY ARE NOT ON MY LIST SO THEY CAN'T COME IN!'
And they'd to jump back in their big posh cars and go!'

Raymond was well suited to his post; he had spent two years in the Coldstream Guards;

'I've done Buckingham Palace and Windsor Castle so that's probably a little bit of experience. Bit different though, guarding the King to guarding a Denby Dale Pie!' he commented in 1988.

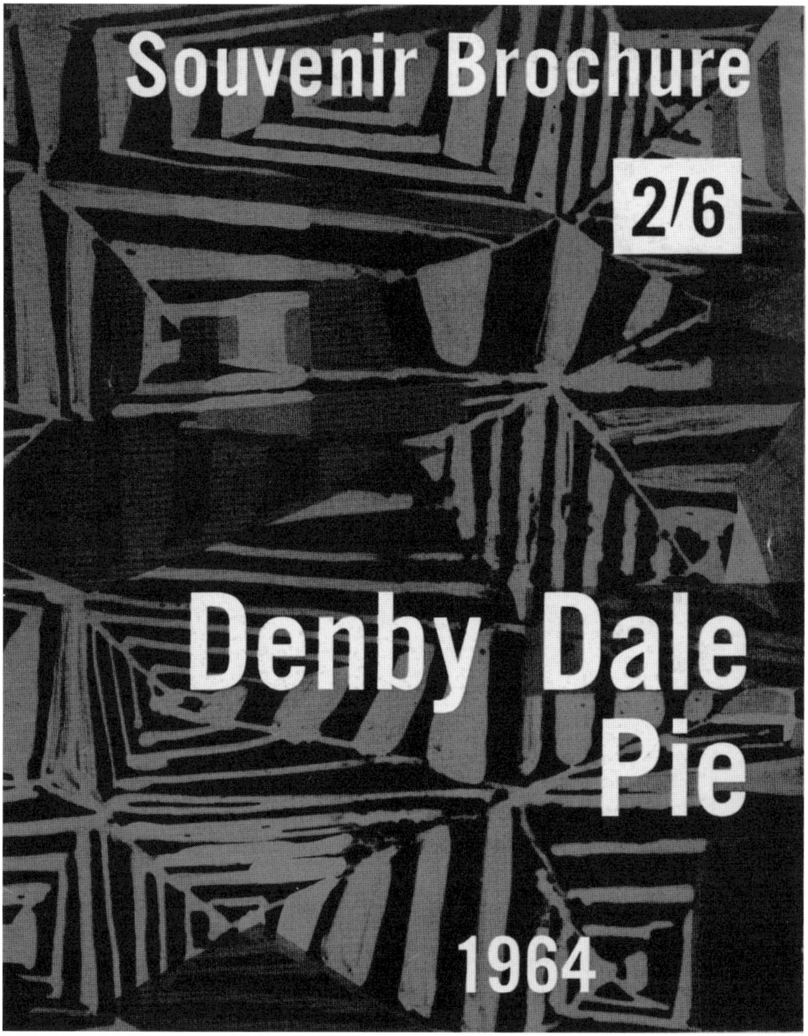

Front cover of the souvenir brochure for the 1964 pie.

For the day to be a success an enormous amount of publicity was required. Before the Committee had even been formed, Mrs Kitson had been interviewed on television regarding her intentions to bake another pie. Press releases were despatched instigating calls from National Newspapers, and then Frank Dale of the popular BBC programme 'Tonight' came to the village. The resulting film took 2 days to shoot,

Fife Robertson watching Mr George Saville baking a trial pie.

lasted nearly a quarter of an hour and included footage from Brian Kitson's engineering works where welding was taking place on the dish itself. Fife Robertson provided the commentary for the film although his car ended up in the wars somewhat!

From the Souvenir Brochure 1964, by John Netherwood:

> *'In the course of the film, Fife Robertson tasted some pie from a twenty pound miniature baked by George Saville at his shop in Upper Denby. Afterwards we all sat down in the George Inn across the road to eat this massive miniature. Whilst we were eating someone came in to ask if the owner of a new white Ford Consul would move his motorcar. This car turned out to belong to Fife Robertson himself. Not wishing to disturb his meal, one of us 'Dalers' (who shall remain nameless) offered to move the car for him. Unfortunately the brewery wagon had just been delivering barrels of ale and had left the planks off the cellarway. Down went the Robertson Consul. The unfortunate driver now has the title of 'im as put Fife Robertson's motor down t'beer 'ole'.*

Although its initial broadcast was delayed by the assassination of American President, John F. Kennedy, the film set the ball rolling. Press cuttings came from many countries, including the Montreal Star. Dated Thursday December 31st, 1963, the headline was 'Biggest Pie of all Time To Be Made In Yorkshire', and information was even requested from Teheran.

A publicity stunt was set up outside the Ship Inn at Mirfield. The Pie dish, assorted furniture and people underneath a canopy, was launched into the river. Seventy three members of the press turned up to report on the story and, even when later that night someone sank the dish, the Committee proved that there is no such thing as bad publicity. Eventually, due to demand, the Committee employed a Public Relations firm as the work became too much for them.

The final event involved the tasting of four pie recipes by a group of distinguished experts including Clement Freud and Philip Harben. They pronounced that the best-tasting combination of spices was number FD895, though the recipe is kept a village secret.

Hopes of a profit of £25,000 were high, estimates of possible crowds ranged from 90,000 to 250,000 though these proved to be highly wild and probably deterred some people from coming. After so much hard work and with so much achieved, the outlook was positive...then tragedy struck.

From the Sheffield Telegraph dated 1st September 1964:

'The world famous Denby Dale Pie ceremony will go on as planned on Saturday, in spite of an accident which killed four of the main organisers. Press officer, Mr John Netherwood, said "The Pie day celebrations will go ahead. When we heard the news we visited all the relatives of the four dead men and asked them whether they thought the celebrations should be cancelled. But

in each and every case the relatives said the event should still be held".

News of the fatal crash stunned the bunting and flag decorated Yorkshire village and Union Jacks flew at half-mast above the wool-mill chimneys.

The four men were killed when the car was involved in a collision with the rear of a 17-ton articulated lorry at the Southern end of the Grantham by-pass in the early hours of yesterday.

They were returning from London, where they had been recording a television programme about the Denby Dale Pie with Eammon Andrews. The dead men were, Mr John Schofield (Chairman of the Pie Planning Committee), Mr George Saville (in charge of the Cooks preparing the Pie and also the baker of the miniature pies from which the ingredients were chosen), Mr Lawrence Wainwright (member of Denby Dale Band who, being the only surviving member of the Band who played at the 1928 festivities, was to have held place of honour in the Saturday procession), and Mr Benny Beever (who was acting as advisor to the Pie committee and who had attended the 1887,1896 & 1928 Pies).

Mr Raymond Haigh, who had taken the Pie dish to London to be filmed for the programme, passed the scene of the accident without realising who was involved.'

On Pie day itself the huge crowds in attendance paid due respect to these four men, falling into silence as the hymn 'Sandon' was played in their memory.

As the day approached, many of the houses in the village and along the route of the procession were decorated; even the viaduct was trimmed with illuminations. The railway line, which was due to have been closed down 3 months before the advent of the Pie, had been kept open and would remain open for 4 days after the end of the proceedings.

In the field behind the White Hart Inn, there was a Wrestling Showring featuring bouts, including the famous Jim Breaks, and a bandstand that was to be used continuously for eight hours, along with a refreshment marquee. Across the road from there was a fairground and the venue for the grand finale of fireworks.

Up in Norman Park there were two more bandstands, the main refreshments bar, a trade fair and, of course, the site for the arrival and distribution of the Pie.

Minutes before the pie was due to start its journey, butcher Mr Jack Hirst raised a cheer from the hundreds jostling outside the barn by announcing ‘It’s ready....... and it’s champion’.

The pie procession passing through the middle of Denby Dale. The back of the White Hart Inn (now Mr. Boons) can be seen in the right of the picture. (Author unknown)

The pie procession in front of the Prospect public house (now The Dalesman), further up Wakefield Road than the preceding picture. Courtesy of Mr B. Heath.

The huge crowd makes its way down Norman Road towards the pie field. Courtesy of Mr B. Heath.

At 2pm the pie left Hector Buckley's milking parlour under a striped canopy. It was drawn by a traction engine called the 'Marshall Foch', owned by the Hunts of the company Specialoid Pistons. Behind came a half-mile long procession of cooks and floats. Miller Hill was safely negotiated and the parade made its way along High Street amidst a huge crowd. The Yorkshire Evening Post noted that:

> *'The Pie was preceded by brass bands and pipe bands playing different tunes – but who cared? - and escorted by six West Riding policemen on prancing horses'.*

A slight hiccup occurred when the canopy of the trailer above the pie collided with overhead power cables, but these were quickly lifted to allow the pie access into its special enclosure in Norman Park. At 3.05pm the Pie was blessed and at 3.15pm Mr Jonas Kenyon performed the cutting ceremony.

The 1964 pie having just arrived at the pie field on the transporting wagon. Courtesy of Mr J.H. Nicholls.

The 'Dalers' put a brave face on for the day though all were mindful of the four men who were not there. The Denby Dale Band started proceedings by playing Abide With Me at the War Memorial bandstand whilst respectful villagers stood to attention and, as already noted, 'Sandon' was played in the Pie field.

In his speech, Jonas Kenyon said:

> *'If, as the result of today's effort, we can build in Denby Dale a Village Hall as a centre of activities it will give the opportunity to regain and maintain a spirit of unity in the village, the same solid and independent spirit which animated this district a generation ago'.*

The pie was served to over 30,000 people and, once the funfair and dance had been sampled, a firework display rounded off the day and with it, success.

The final amount raised from Pie day was £6,573.10s.2d. This, along with other fund raising ventures and interest accrued, increased to nearly £10,000, which was matched by a grant from the Department of Education through the Yorkshire Rural Community Council.

In late 1969, the Pie Committee purchased Birkwood House in the centre of Denby Dale, together with a piece of land adjoining it. The house was converted into the desired Village Hall for £23,847.00. It was opened on 5th September 1972, exactly eight years after the Pie day itself. Inside, a plaque was erected on the wall in memoriam of the four Committee members killed in the fateful car crash only days before the event in 1964. Today, the Hall is used by such groups as the Women's Institute, Darby & Joan Club, The Amateur Radio Club, Flower Club, Keep Fit Classes and Old Time Dancing. None of the groups pay a hire fee but give the Pie Hall a donation each year in accordance with their available resources.

The pie dish remains there to this day taking pride of place in the car park and acting as a raised flowerbed!

The Bicentenary Pie - Pie Number Nine (3rd September 1988)

The village of Denby Dale had seen many changes since the first recorded Pie festivities in 1788/9. Most notable was the growth and subsequently rapid demise of its industry.

By 1988 only one of the three large textile manufacturers was left. Jonas Kenyon and the Brownhill Group had ceased trading, leaving only Z. Hinchliffe & Sons as a mass employer in the village. The Corn Mill at the bottom of Miller Hill was demolished by 1975 and replaced by new housing, the estate now being called Brookside.

In 1976 the old school had closed and moved to a new site at Gilthwaites, and the village as a whole had become a residential area playing its part in the commuter age.

The traditional close-knit ties within the village community had all but evaporated, but towards the end of 1985 a group of meetings occurred with a view to turning back the clock and celebrating the village's famous traditions in the only style possible.

A new Pie Committee was formed which decided that the celebrations should be held in 1988 to commemorate 200 years of Pie making in the village. A monster pie to celebrate baking monster pies!

To generate funds for expenses incurred along the way, fund-raising events were organised, including a Halloween Dance and Cheese and Wine luncheon, and 200 people attended a barbecue. These were followed in 1987 by a Human Horse Race Night and a Fashion Show which attracted more than 400 people.

The venture achieved charitable status and officially launched the baking of a Pie on the 18th March 1987, the date for the big day being 3rd September 1988. The Committee decided that the celebrations should continue into the Sunday; a two-day festival to commemorate 200 years.

The Committee wasted no time in swinging into action. Pie memorabilia was commissioned, including launch-night plates as well as the usual well-established plates. A touring caravan, known as the Denby Dale Pie Roadshow travelled far and wide promoting the big day. A float was prepared for the Denby Dale Carnival '87 and a Post Office Box was acquired to allow the public to write for up to date information.

It was also in 1987 that Billington Structures, of Wombwell, Barnsley agreed to build and sponsor the Pie dish. Made of mild steel and measuring 20ft by 7ft, by $1^1/_2$ ft deep, it weighed around half a ton and was designed to hold seven cubic metres of Pie. Estimated contents for the pie were:

3,000kg of prime English beef, 3,000kg of potatoes, 700kg of onions, 700kg of gravy and spices, 1,500kg of flour and 1,200kg of margarine – whilst in early 1988 scholars at Scissett Middle School planted potatoes and onions which, when harvested, were to be used in the pie.

The Pie was to be the biggest ever and should be able to serve 50,000 people, but since 1964 a lot of the rules had changed. Methods of cooking, suitable ingredients and utensils, parading and serving the Pie were balanced by a need to comply with Environmental Health requirements. Luckily members of that Government department were very supportive but, to comply with regulations, the floor of the barn at Upper Denby was lined with polythene and specially treated to make sure that no dust could rise.

The cooking was done as follows:

The process consists of the meat filling being cooked in steam kettles in $^1/_4$ tonne batches, and filled into 12 trays contained within one big tray. Circulating hot

water around and within the small trays will maintain the required temperature. Heat losses are controlled by suitable insulation.
The parading of the Pie will take approximately an hour, after which it will be connected to another hot water generator to maintain the contents at serving temperature. During the parade the residual heat and the insulation will ensure that the temperature does not fall below the critical level. During the parade a levelling system utilising air-jacks will be used to overcome the gradients along the route.

[From the Souvenir Pie 88 Brochure]

Ahmed Pochee, a Laboratory Manager for a Flour Confectionery Manufacturer, was in charge of these activities.

Besides the fun aspects of promoting the Pie, such as choosing the Bicentenary Pie Queen, (a position filled ably by Miss Janet Armitage, at that time aged 16 and a student at Shelley High School) it was also necessary to consider traffic and parking problems that would undoubtedly arise on the day. The Committee placed great emphasis on the use of public transport and a Pie Rover Metro ticket was produced for the

The pie field on the Barnsley Road, looking from Miller Hill.

day, whilst bus and rail timetables were adjusted and altered so that the services would pass the Pie field.

Local farmers donated their land to provide car parking to facilitate a Park and Ride operation subsidised by the Pie Trust. Police, Environmental Health and the St. John Ambulance and West Yorkshire Ambulance Services were also consulted. Massive crowds were expected to attend the first two-day Denby Dale Pie.

A circular was produced by West Yorkshire Police, asking all local residents for co-operation in keeping roads clear, and informing them of restrictions. The event was policed by 100 full and part-time officers, aided by special constables and a helicopter.

Publicity for the event was featured on both Radio and Television. Martin Wiley narrated 'The Big Pie' on Radio Leeds, which included interviews with some of the 1988 Trustee's; Raymond Haigh, pie historian David Bostwick and old 'Daler', the late Joseph Peace. The BBC made a half-hour documentary, narrated by Harry Gration, which presented a brief history of the Pies and culminated with footage taken during the 1988 event. The programme was broadcast the following week.

The pie leaving Upper Denby. The George Inn is in the background.

Part of the procession for the 1988 pie, showing representations of the past pie dishes.

During the week before the big day, heavy rain had waterlogged the Pie field site on Barnsley Road and had left the organisers with a few headaches. Press officer, Barrie Clarke, admitted that on the Friday ‘the outlook had seemed bleak’, and that ‘it had not done much for our enthusiasm when a television presenter who visited the field on Friday night described the site as a “washed-out, windswept spot”.’

As tents and marquees began to go up, interest and anticipation increased. The Funfair arrived and little by little the rain-sodden mud baths that had been fields gradually yielded to the tractors hauling in the lorries and equipment. Hopes grew when the weather forecast for the weekend held an improvement. This first two-day extravaganza desperately needed good weather to succeed.

Events for the Saturday, aside from the Pie, were Pipe Bands, an Escapologist, a Parachute Drop and a Chinese Lion Dance. Children were catered for with a Bouncy Castle, a Baby Elephant and Pickles the Clown! Radio Leeds would be making regular broadcasts from the Pie field and in other areas were Steam Engines, a Hot Air Balloon, Army Bikes and a

The procession passing the Prospect public house (now the Dalesman) in Wakefield Road.

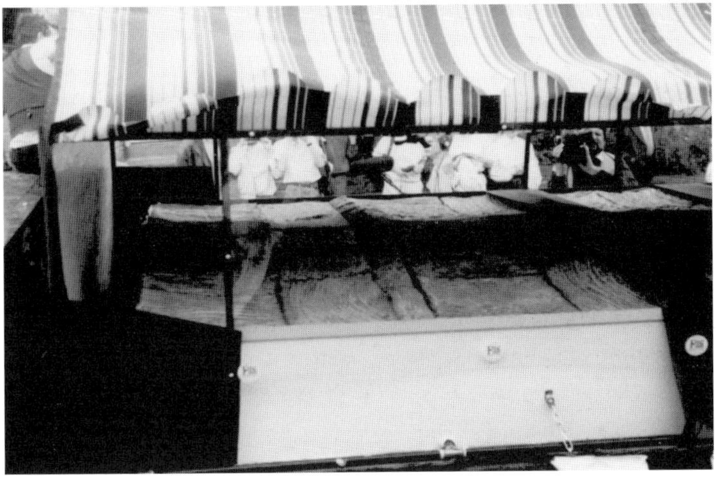

Close up view of the pie, showing the squares of pastry on top.

Helicopter Pad (for flights over the pie field). The day was due to finish with a Fireworks Display.

Sunday was almost as good. Besides a Donkey Derby, another Parachute Drop, Morris Dancers and an RSPCA dog show, the Radio 1 Roadshow and its host, Mike Read, were going to be broadcasting live to the nation from the pie field. An awful lot hinged on the weather...

Showing the massive queues at the serving tent.

Inside the serving tent.

On Saturday morning the sun was shining; the Gods were on the side of the Pie '88 Trust. The Pie left its oven at Upper Denby a little after midday. Cooking had gone well. A small crowd witnessed the lorry, belonging to R.J.Tait & Son, haul the monster pie, covered by a blue and white canopy, into Bank

Lane. From there it went on into Denby Lane and down the hill towards the Dunkirk Public House, where the crowds of people waiting were being entertained by Hade Edge Band. The trailer carrying the pie had sixteen wheels to enable it to carry its load of more than seven tons. Driven by Susan Ross, it made its way down into the decorated village, safely negotiating Miller Hill, and then turned left into Wakefield Road where the crowds were thickest. Joining it were the members of a massive, mile-long procession that included the traction engine used to draw the 1964 Pie, along with Scouts, Morris Dancers, Floats, Brass Bands, a Scottish Pipe Band and people in fancy dress.

Two tractors helped the pie's entry into the muddy, hard-core covered conditions of the Pie field, and painfully slowly it reached its destination. The Mayor of Kirklees, Clr. John Holt, raised three cheers for the Pie and then the Bishop of Pontefract, the Rt. Rev. Richard Hare, said Grace. John Hinchliffe, Chairman of the 1964 Pie committee, who had been chosen to perform the ceremonial First Cut into the Pie was

The pie festival in full swing on Sunday, the second day, with the Radio 1 Roadshow in the background.

handed 2ft long Servers by the Chairman of the Pie Trust, Graham Fussey. Mr Fussey thanked the Committee for their efforts and joked that; 'As well as a lot of hard work being involved, there was also a lot of meat and potato'. After a short speech Mr Hinchliffe cut open the crust.

The team of 170 servers was quickly in business and people paid £1 for a 4oz portion of pie with crust, decorated cardboard plate and plastic utensils. The pie was deemed to be good. Indeed, Local MP Ann Taylor (currently Leader of the House), described the Pie as 'absolutely delicious'. It was over two hours before the lengthy queues began to subside.

Despite all the hard work by the Trust, there were many problems on the day. Traffic congestion resulted in long waits for the advertised free Park and Ride services, both coming and going to the Pie field. Many people gatecrashed the festivities as the only entrance to the field was swamped with people. Walls were broken down as crowds swept into the field free of charge, prompting the police and marshals to guard certain sections of the ground. Police placed the crowd figures at 100,000 on the first day, which was followed up on the second day with a further 50,000 who attended the Radio 1 Roadshow and all the other activities. Despite all this there were no arrests and no major incidents.

The Pie entered the Guinness Book of Records as the biggest Meat and Potato Pie in the world, beating the previous record held by the Americans, although a somewhat larger Apple Pie still held the overall record, again made by the Americans.

The event had been expected to raise a large amount of money for local charities and projects. Initially, however, it made a loss estimated to be in the region of £40,000. An official investigation was launched, but was unable to find sufficient evidence to warrant further action.

The major problem was that the amount of money that had been banked could not be reconciled with the portions of pie sold and ticket receipts. Of course, the many gatecrashers who avoided the £2 entrance fee to the field did not help matters. The worst aspect of the inquiry was the shadow of suspicion under which the Trustees had to live, particularly considering all their hard work and time.

To their credit, they overturned the losses and eventually made a profit of £8,000. This was achieved through further sales of memorabilia and the settlement of a dispute over an account with a public relations company. The money was used to purchase Wither Wood at the top of the Gilthwaites housing estate in the village, to preserve it for the community and protect it against any development. The Pie dish itself now forms part of a Butterfly Garden at Gilthwaites First School, its great girth filled with plants to help create an attractive garden.

There is no doubt that the Pie celebrations in 1988 were a success. It was suggested, during the euphoria at the time, that a Pie might be baked to celebrate the millennium. It would seem, however, that the hard work involved, the months of planning, the time and the cost, have deterred thoughts to this end.

The village tradition has not died though, it is simply lying dormant, an almost mythological monster of immense proportions which appears, maybe, only once a generation, roused by the voices of a fanatical (and some would say idiotic!) few. As the monster rises like a Phoenix from the embers of the last pie it begins to spread its wings. The voices increase, breeding cherished memories of bygone days, until the clamour is almost deafening and the village of Denby Dale can only slay the beast by baking another Pie.

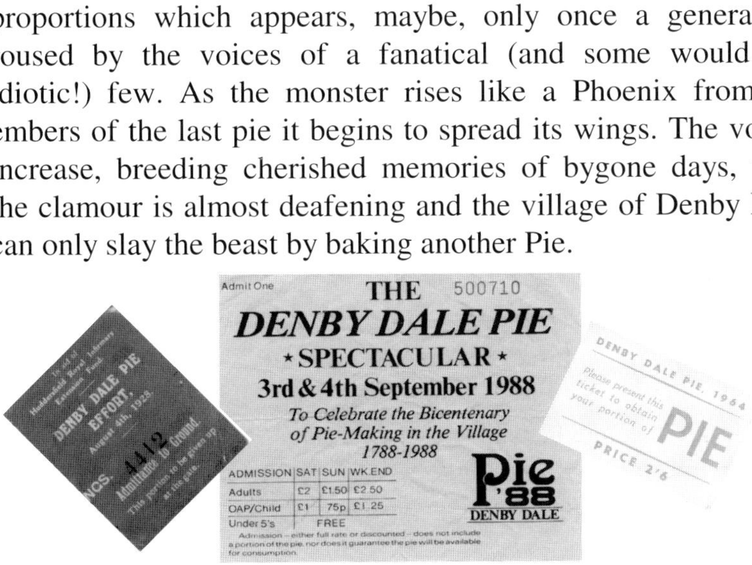

THE
DENBY DALE
1788
1988
BICENTENARY PIE
Souvenir Brochure £1

PART TWO

Memorabilia of the Denby Dale Pies

Among the many interesting and unique features of the baking of a Denby Dale Pie, is the merchandise made commercially available to raise funds in order to account for expenses in the planning and organisation, and also to aid eventual profits. Alongside this are the numerous non-commercial souvenirs collected by the public, legally or otherwise, which have passed down from generation to generation as heirlooms. Many adding value to their collectability throughout the years.

The 'Huddersfield Examiner' reported in August 1928:

"RELICS OF THE GREAT DENBY DALE PIE - Sold by Auction:

In Denby Dale Council School the relics of the great Carnival Pie, utensils that were used in its making and a number of other lots associated with the effort for the Huddersfield Royal Infirmary, were offered for sale by public auction.

Mr G H Wilby was the auctioneer, but there was little conventional about the sale. No restrictions were read out and the Incorporated Law Society was not called to witness. The rule appeared to be that the highest bidder was most certainly the buyer.

The first article offered was a large tin bath. About this the auctioneer waxed eloquent. 'Was it not used in the most stupendous effort that has ever been made in Denby Dale on behalf of charity?' he asked.

But the bids came slowly. After all, a large tin bath, however useful it may be as a bath, is hardly the thing that people would choose as a souvenir. But then the auctioneer pointed out that in this very bath, part of the great pie had been carried before being served to the waiting thousands. That did it, and Mr Arthur Brook acquired the lot for 6s 9d.

Next came an artistic metal vessel, decorated in simple manner in white and blue enamel. People with no poetry in their souls called it a tin bowl but Mr Wilby asked that this lot should not be priced as if it were being bought in a shop. This too had associations with the pie that added many times to its value. Mrs Blamires parted with 3s 6d.

'Ladles, three assorted' was the next item and the first ones to be put up complete with handles.

'This', said the auctioneer, 'simply wants a little decoration, and then think of it's value as a decorative article in any front room. What will it be worth in a hundred years time?'

'Yes, what?' somebody asked doubtfully.

But bidding commenced briskly and rose rapidly from 1s to £1 when they were sold to Mr W. Dewhirst. This was the highest price raised by a single article during the sale. Smaller ladles were then offered for 6s apiece. Six shillings was also the price realised for the dripping tin, which still bore the marks of its encounter with the giant pie, and which the connoisseurs who were present had to admit was indeed beautifully marked.

Several real gems, which were eagerly sought by the bidders, had been saved until the latter part of the sale. There was a perfect specimen of a paper doily, in all probability of the early Woolworth dynasty. Upon this doily the first piece of pie was served, and on it too was to be seen the mark of the time. Mrs Jonas Kenyon was the purchaser at 2s 6d.

Mrs Kenyon was presented with a meat hook used in fastening the muslin over the edges of the pie in recognition of her services.

By this time interest had begun to flag, but everybody revived when the auctioneer announced that he had to offer a cricket bat, won as a boy by Mr Harry Turton at the sports in connection with the baking of the Jubilee pie in 1887. This fetched 14s and a programme of events for the same celebrations made 7s 6d.

When a signed agenda, calling together a meeting in connection with the barrel organ collections, was sold to a gentleman from another village, there was almost as great a sensation as when the manuscript of 'Alice in Wonderland' was knocked down to an American buyer some months ago.

Then there was the half of the paste medallion, which the auctioneer described as forming 'The culminating point of the whole structure', in other words, it was the piece of crust that was situated in the middle of the pie. It was sold with a certificate certifying it to be genuine, and signed by the five ladies who placed it there on the great day. Mr Jubb, who was the buyer, estimated the value of the piece of crust at 4s, and the signatures of the ladies at sixpence.

Several people were disappointed that they could not secure bargains, but none more so than the man who spoke to me at the door;

'I'm sorry that they didn't put up the dish for sale', he said.

'Why?' I asked,

'Well, I wanted a pond for my ducks', was his reply."

The things that people will pay good money for! The term 'Piemania' has been coined, and it would certainly appear to have begun at least this far back, but then consider again the amount of crusts or slices that have been preserved by local families for years.

During the chaos of 1846, trophy hunters were in action. As the pie was being torn to shreds and trampled under-foot, some far-sighted individuals managed to grab pieces of the crust, which have been preserved to this day! Similarly, pieces also survive from 1887, 1896, 1928 and 1964. Indeed, local farmer the late Mr Tom Lodge, was featured on the BBC documentary of 1988 at his home at Toby Wood farm, where he proudly removed from his freezer a piece of the 1964 pie, retained from that day.

It may sound strange to the outsider, but owning a piece of a bygone pie is a prestigious accolade to be treasured and revered. Indeed, when asked by children or outsiders, the locals would invariably give the wrong directions as to the location of the 'grave' of the Jubilee pie so as to prevent them digging up a piece to keep as a souvenir for themselves.

As we have seen, items associated with the advertising, cooking or distribution of a pie were also highly prized. Banners, signposts, tickets, cutlery, bunting, you name it, and you can almost guarantee that somewhere something has survived!

It was in 1887 that the beginnings of a by now well established tradition took root. The first Pie Plate was produced, bearing a portrait of Queen Victoria in the centre and having the words, 'Souvenir, Denby Dale Pie, 8 feet diameter and 2 feet deep, Queen's Jubilee 1887', and the date 'August 27 1887', emblazoned on it. Produced to promote and celebrate a successful day, they were balanced by the 'Funeral Cards' printed hurriedly for its burial in Toby Wood, three days after the event. A good number of these Funeral Cards survive, but are highly sought after by collectors of pie souvenirs.

The commemorative plate for the 1887 pie.
Courtesy of the Tolson Museum, Huddersfield.

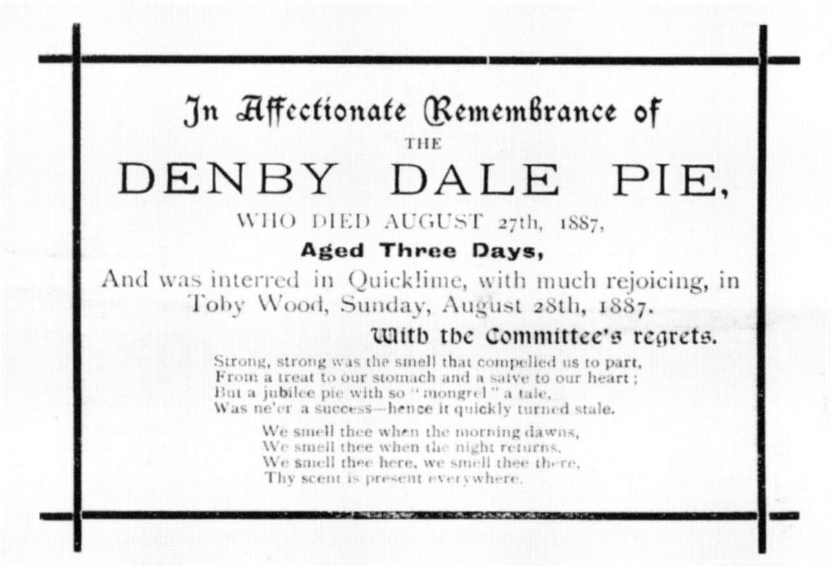

In Affectionate Remembrance of
THE
DENBY DALE PIE,
WHO DIED AUGUST 27th, 1887,
Aged Three Days,
And was interred in Quicklime, with much rejoicing, in Toby Wood, Sunday, August 28th, 1887.

With the Committee's regrets.

Strong, strong was the smell that compelled us to part,
From a treat to our stomach and a salve to our heart;
But a jubilee pie with so "mongrel" a tale,
Was ne'er a success—hence it quickly turned stale.

We smell thee when the morning dawns,
We smell thee when the night returns,
We smell thee here, we smell thee there,
Thy scent is present everywhere.

Another two examples of Memorial Cards produced for the burial of the 1887 pie. A previous example was shown on page 15.
Courtesy of the Tolson Museum, Huddersfield.

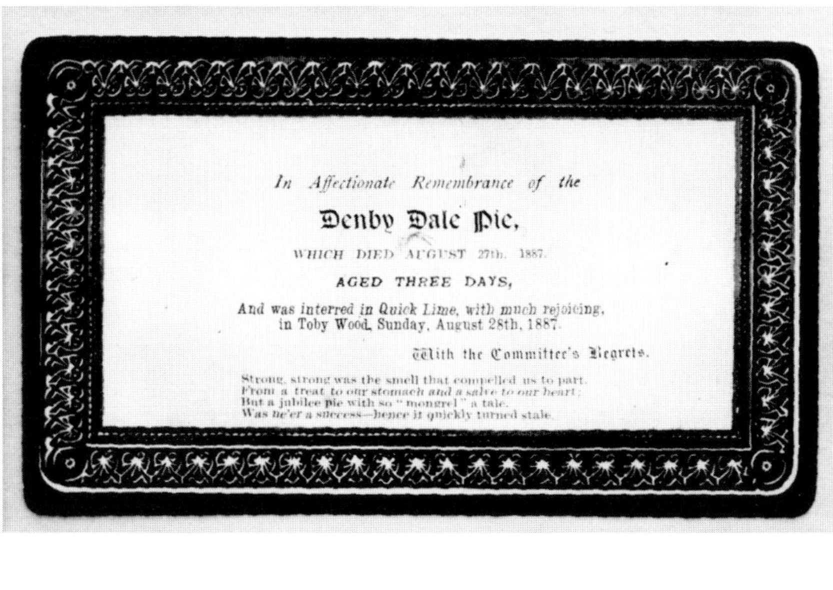

In Affectionate Remembrance of the
Denby Dale Pie,
WHICH DIED AUGUST 27th. 1887.
AGED THREE DAYS,
And was interred in Quick Lime, with much rejoicing, in Toby Wood, Sunday, August 28th, 1887.

With the Committee's Regrets.

Strong, strong was the smell that compelled us to part,
From a treat to our stomach and a salve to our heart;
But a jubilee pie with so "mongrel" a tale,
Was ne'er a success—hence it quickly turned stale.

An example of the rarer 1887 plate, showing the two portraits of Victoria. Courtesy of the Tolson Museum, Huddersfield.

Astonishingly, another plate was produced for the Resurrection Pie a week later. Now a very rare commodity, these plates bore two portraits of the Queen, one as she was at the beginning of her reign and the other as she was at the time of the baking of the pie. The plates sold well, but one could speculate that their rarity could be due to low production numbers caused by time constraints.

Pie plates were now coming thick and fast. Another was produced for the celebrations of 1896 and was similar in concept, though the portrait of Queen Victoria was now replaced by a painting of a pie, which looked very much like a pork pie of today. The words around the rim were:

'Denby Dale, Jubilee Pie In Commemoration of the Repeal of the Corn Laws 1846'.

The 1896 plate commemorating the repeal of the Corn Laws.
Courtesy of Mr & Mrs J. H. Nicholls.

Also produced was a silver brooch, more commonly known as a pie-pin. It is unknown at present how many of these were made, but a local newspaper cutting reported the following:

> *'Miscellany has had another couple of calls about the silver pie pins issued to mark the 1896 Denby Dale pie. One lady phoned to say that her family had kept a pin in a button box, but it was now resting in a safer place. She understood that three pins were made at the time. But then a lady wrote from Bradford to say that she also had a pin which, like the others, had been handed down from older members of the family. So we are now wondering just how many pie pins were made'.*

The answer is certainly more than three. My own Uncle also possesses one, and the article obviously makes reference to others still in existence. The brooch itself was fashioned

The silver brooch or 'Pie-pin' produced for the 1896 pie. Pictured approximately three times actual size. Courtesy of Mr R. Heath.

into the shape of a pie, surrounded by a neat floral design. It gives the date of the pie and its dimensions. It is to be wondered just how many more still survive, buried in button boxes or packed away in drawers or lofts?

Programmes were also issued for the 1846 Pie. Priced at one penny each, the single page gave details about the contents of the pie, its dimensions and its weight.

The 1928-pie plate adopted a similar theme to that of its predecessor, a glazed white plate, with the words, 'Denby Dale Pie In Aid of the Huddersfield Royal Infirmary'. In the middle was another painting of a pie, (though this one was steaming hot!) and, of course, the necessary dimensions. A special edition of the plate was made for the Committee members, bearing an inner border of red, blue and green leaves as well as the above-described design.

David Bostwick also noted that:

'Besides plates a few special dinner services were manufactured, with oval meat dishes, covered tureens and gravy boats, all bearing the steaming pie design'.

The latter, along with the special edition plate, are now very rare and much sought after by collectors.

Also in existence from this time are many printed poems and songs, composed to celebrate the day's events in verse, such as the following, which was to be sung to the tune of 'Cranbrook', perhaps better known as 'On Ilkla Moor Bah't 'at':

(Repeat the last two lines of each verse)

Of Woodland Dale, proud Denby Dale,
We sing the song and shout the Tale,
When Wellington, victor home did sail,
They made a pie at T'Dale.

Of Woodland Dale, proud Denby Dale,
We sing the song and shout the Tale,
When folks could reach the Dale by rail,
Pie platform broke at T'Dale.

Of Woodland Dale, proud Denby Dale,
We sing the song and shout the Tale,
Two Pies were made for one was stale,
Victoria's reign to hail.

Of Woodland Dale, proud Denby Dale,
We sing the song and shout the Tale,
For half a century's free food sale,
Huge Pie we made at T'Dale.

Of Woodland Dale, proud Denby Dale,
We sing the song and shout the Tale,
A thousand pounds they want to mail,
From the Council's Pie at T'Dale.

The sheets, printed by Hirst Buckley of Scissett, contained two other songs and cost 1d each, the proceeds all going towards the total to be given to the Huddersfield Royal Infirmary.

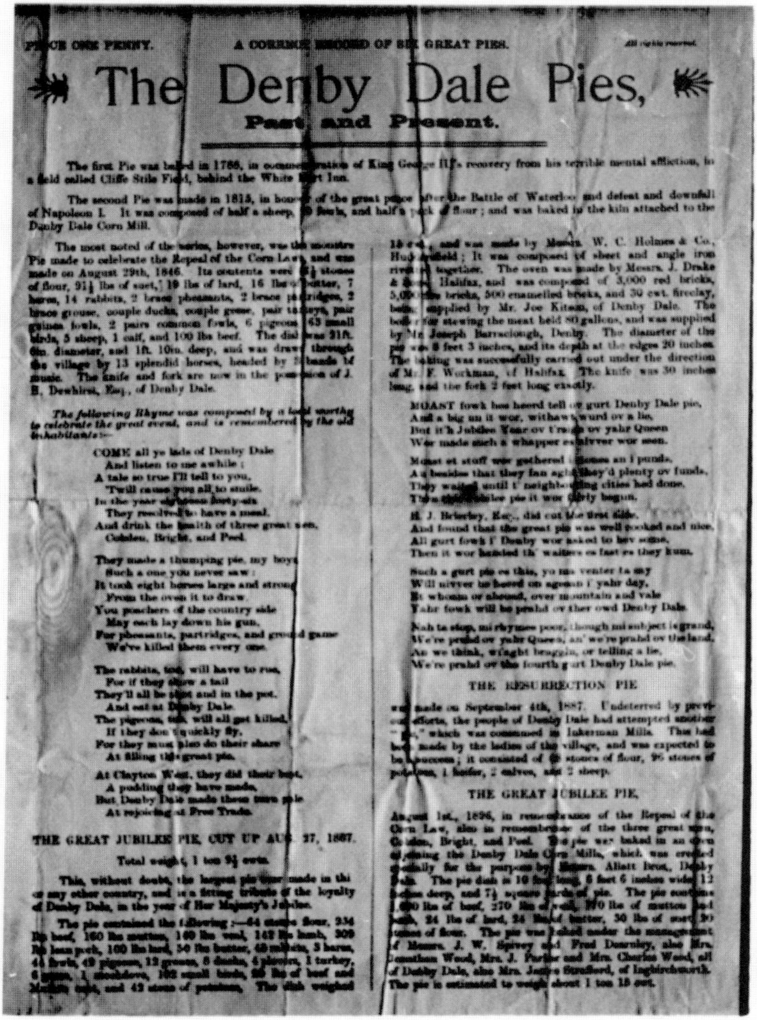

PRICE ONE PENNY. A CORRECT RECORD OF SIX GREAT PIES. All rights reserved.

The Denby Dale Pies,

Past and Present.

The first Pie was baked in 1788, in commemoration of King George III.'s recovery from his terrible mental affliction, in a field called Cliffe Stile Field, behind the White Hart Inn.

The second Pie was made in 1815, in honour of the great peace after the Battle of Waterloo and defeat and downfall of Napoleon I. It was composed of half a sheep, 20 fowls, and half a peck of flour; and was baked in the kiln attached to the Denby Dale Corn Mill.

The most noted of the series, however, was the monstre Pie made to celebrate the Repeal of the Corn Laws, and was made on August 29th, 1846. Its contents were 5½ stones of flour, 91½ lbs of suet, 19 lbs of lard, 16 lbs of butter, 7 hares, 14 rabbits, 2 brace pheasants, 2 brace partridges, 2 brace grouse, couple ducks, couple geese, pair turkeys, pair guinea fowls, 2 pairs common fowls, 6 pigeons, 63 small birds, 5 sheep, 1 calf, and 100 lbs beef. The dish was 21ft. 6in. diameter, and 1ft. 10in. deep, and was drawn through the village by 13 splendid horses, headed by 3 bands of music. The knife and fork are now in the possession of J. B. Dewhirst, Esq., of Denby Dale.

The following Rhyme was composed by a local worthy to celebrate the great event, and is remembered by the old inhabitants:—

COME all ye lads of Denby Dale
And listen to me awhile;
A tale so true I'll tell to you,
'Twill cause you all to smile.
In the year eighteen forty-six
They resolved to have a meal,
And drink the health of three great men,
Cobden, Bright, and Peel.

They made a thumping pie, my boys,
Such a one you never saw:
It took eight horses large and strong
From the oven it to draw.
You poachers of the country side
May each lay down his gun,
For pheasants, partridges, and ground game
We've killed them every one.

The rabbits, too, will have to run,
For if they show a tail
They'll all be shot and in the pot,
And eat at Denby Dale.
The pigeons, too, will all get killed,
If they don't quickly fly,
For they must also do their share
At filling this great pie.

At Clayton West, they did their best,
A pudding they have made,
But Denby Dale made them a pie
At rejoicing at Free Trade.

THE GREAT JUBILEE PIE, CUT UP AUG. 27, 1887.

Total weight, 1 ton 9¼ cwts.

This, without doubt, the largest pie ever made in this or any other country, and is a fitting tribute of the loyalty of Denby Dale, in the year of Her Majesty's Jubilee.

The pie contained the following:—64 stones flour, 336 lbs beef, 160 lbs mutton, 160 lbs veal, 147 lbs lamb, 309 lbs lean pork, 100 lbs lard, 50 lbs butter, 40 rabbits, 3 hares, 46 fowls, 49 pigeons, 12 grouse, 8 ducks, 4 plovers, 1 turkey, 6 geese, 1 woodcock, 102 small birds, 60 lbs of beef and Mutton suet, and 42 stone of potatoes. The dish weighed 15 cwt., and was made by Messrs. W. C. Holmes & Co., Huddersfield; It was composed of sheet and angle iron rivetted together. The oven was made by Messrs. J. Drake & Sons, Halifax, and was composed of 3,000 red bricks, 5,000 [illegible] bricks, 500 enamelled bricks, and 30 cwt. fireclay, being supplied by Mr. Joe Kitson, of Denby Dale. The boiler for stewing the meat held 80 gallons, and was supplied by Mr. Joseph Barraclough, Denby. The diameter of the pie was 8 feet 3 inches, and its depth at the edges 20 inches. The baking was successfully carried out under the direction of Mr. F. Workman, of Halifax. The knife was 30 inches long, and the fork 2 feet long exactly.

MOAST fowk hes heerd tell ov gurt Denby Dale pie,
An' a big un it wor, withaht a wurd ov a lie,
But i'th Jubilee Year ov t'reign ov yahr Queen
Wor made sich a whapper as niver wor seen.

Moast ot stuff wor gethered i' stones an i' punds,
An' besides that they fan agin they'd plenty ov funds,
They waited until t' neighbouring cities had done,
Then [illegible] pie it wor fairly begun.

H. J. Brierley, Esq., did cut t' first slice,
And found that the great pie was well cooked and nice,
All gurt fowk i' Denby wor asked to hev some,
Then it wor handed th' waiters as fast as they kum.

Such a gurt pie as this, yo mo venter to say
Will niver be heerd on agean i' yahr day,
Bi whoam or abroad, over mountain and vale
Yahr fowk will be prahd ov ther own Denby Dale.

Nah ta stop, mi rhymes poor, though mi subject is grand,
We're prahd ov yahr Queen, an' we're prahd ov the land,
An we think, wi'aght braggin, or telling a lie,
We're prahd ov the fourth gurt Denby Dale pie.

THE RESURRECTION PIE

was made on September 4th, 1887. Undeterred by previous efforts, the people of Denby Dale had attempted another "pie," which was commenced in Inkerman Mills. This had been made by the ladies of the village, and was expected to be a success; it consisted of 50 stones of flour, 95 stones of potatoes, 1 heifer, 2 calves, and 2 sheep.

THE GREAT JUBILEE PIE,

August 1st., 1896, in remembrance of the Repeal of the Corn Law, also in remembrance of the three great men, Cobden, Bright, and Peel. The pie was baked in an oven adjoining the Denby Dale Corn Mills, which was erected specially for the purpose by Messrs. Allatt Bros., Denby Dale. The pie dish is 10 feet long, 6 feet 6 inches wide, 12 inches deep, and 7½ square yards of pie. The pie contains 1,050 lbs of beef, 270 lbs of veal, 170 lbs of mutton and lamb, 24 lbs of lard, 24 lbs of butter, 30 lbs of suet, 30 stones of flour. The pie was baked under the management of Messrs. J. W. Spivey and Fred Dearnley, also Mrs. Jonathan Wood, Mrs. J. Parker and Mrs. Charles Wood, all of Denby Dale, also Mrs. James Stratford, of Inghirchworth. The pie is estimated to weigh about 1 ton 15 cwt.

A sample of the song sheets and pie history produced for the 1928 pie. Courtesy of the Tolson Museum, Huddersfield.

The 1928 pie plate commemorating the appeal for the Huddersfield Royal Infirmary. Courtesy of Mr & Mrs J. H. Nicholls.

Memorabilia also exists from the auction and subsequent melt down of the 1887/1896 pie dish in 1940. The large, red, black and blue posters advertising the event have survived in many homes and businesses. Indeed, posters and banners from previous and subsequent celebrations are again, treasured items. As we have already seen, a few rusted pieces of the dish were sold separately at the auction, the purchasers being allowed to retain them. Though it would seem, according to David Bostwick, that only one of these pieces still survives.

The Committee of the 1964 pie was not ignorant of the potential marketing possibilities that confronted them. The by now established tradition of producing a Commemorative Plate was duly continued, supplied by Britannia Designs Ltd., of Townstal Pottery, Dartmouth, Devon. The design was chosen from a village competition and once the winner was chosen the Committee placed orders for large quantities.

By July, about 7,000 had already been sold and by August the Sales Committee wrote in 'Pie News' that if you hadn't already bought your Pie Plate – 'don't leave it too late'.

> *'The pottery have told the Committee, in reply to their request for further stocks of plates, that they are unable to produce any more before Pie Day, and it is the general policy that once Sept. 5th is over no more will be ordered, otherwise this job of selling could go on forever. The despatching department is at present getting off an order for 750 plates. The company which has ordered these will send them out to its own customers throughout the world, and attached to each one will be a calendar for 1965'.*

The 1964 plate showing the dates of the previous pies.
Courtesy of Mr & Mrs J. H. Nicholls.

The Committee was also despatching plates by post, world-wide, and was pleased to report that only one had arrived broken with only a month to go before the big day.

Alongside plates, a limited edition of large and small tankards was made, selling for 17/6 and 10/- each. A booklet was produced under the direction of Mrs. Nora Kitson, entitled 'The Mammoth Pies of Denby Dale', priced at 3/-, and this amongst other items, was available to the public at most local shops which had been appointed to sell the souvenirs.

A souvenir brochure, price 2/6, was produced for the day of the pie itself. Besides featuring many interesting adverts for companies not now in existence, there was a history of pie making in the village, written by John Netherwood, and other interesting articles concerning the preparations for this year's happy event.

After a gap of eight years, further memorabilia was produced to celebrate the opening of the Pie Hall in 1972. Commemorative glassware was commissioned, bearing the dates of previous pies as well as the date of this important event.

By 1988 the era of commercialism had been in place for some time and, once the decision had been taken to bake another pie in 1988, the call for commemorative memorabilia went wild.

Committee member, Stan Ward, fashioned an eye-catching logo, which was to feature on all official pie memorabilia. Once more the design for the plates was decided by having a competition. Mr J. Pearson of Penistone beat over seventy other entries and his design was printed on over 30,000 plates by 'Johnson Brothers', part of the Waterford-Wedgewood group in Stoke-on-Trent. The 'Pie Report' gave the following details:

> *'Using a hand-engraving method from a copper plate, the decoration will be underglazed to ensure that it is dishwasher and microwave safe. The shape is traditional sovereign, the plate is of the finest quality earthenware and will be produced in blue and white'.*

For pre-paid advance orders the cost of a plate was £7.50, until the 1st June when the cost was to rise to £8.50, but that was not the only plate of the year!

A plate had already been commissioned to commemorate the launch night back in 1987. It was a limited edition bearing the pie logo in gold, purchased along with mugs from the Hornsea Pottery. Also produced was a plate given to the servers in recognition of their hard work making the total number of plates up to three!

A plate was produced by Goss China in Stoke on Trent bearing a sepia design (by John Ball) depicting different aspects of previous pie celebrations. A 9-inch pie dish, bearing the same design, was produced by Royal Worcester. Sold exclusively through the Peter Jones china shops, the plate cost £12.50 and the dish £13.50.

The plate produced for the 1988 Bicentenary pie.

The limited edition Coalport plate for the 1988 pie. This plate was produced with full colour pictures.

Also commissioned by the Denby Dale Pie Trust from Peter Jones was a limited edition colour plate, which was produced by Coalport. John Ball was again responsible for the artwork on the 10-inch plate, which retailed at £40.00. These are now collector's items as only 2,000 were produced, and were available in the pie field on pie day as well as at Peter Jones' outlets.

The polystyrene dishes, which would be used to serve up the pie, bore a design chosen from entries by local schoolchildren, and so, in 1988 everyone had a chance to be part of history!

By the time of the official launch-night, hats, balloons, pens and stickers had been ordered. These were followed by mugs, matches, glassware, combs, keyrings and postcards. A local company, Cellarchoice, supplied wine from the Loire Valley in France. Both red and white wines were marketed in specially designed bottles. Instead of paper labels, the history of 'Pie Madness' and the pie '88 logo were enamelled onto the bottles and, again, many have been kept as souvenirs.

A song was also recorded for the big day. Written and performed by local close harmony group, Take Five, it was paired with the Holmfirth Anthem, Pratty Flowers. Although not a serious challenger for a Number 1 position, it added in fine style to the growing stacks of memorabilia already available.

Two books were also written. Locally born David Bostwick, who for many years was Honorary Curator of Pie Memorabilia on behalf of the Pie Hall, wrote an excellent illustrated history of the Pies. He also aided in T.V. and Radio publicity. Additionally, children's author Helen Cresswell had her story, “The Piemakers”, based on the history of the pie, re-issued by publishers Faber & Faber to coincide with the 1988 event.

All of these souvenir items, along with cuddly toys and sweatshirts, were sold from the pie shop at Springfield Mills, in the village, from December 1987.

Of course, certain individuals and companies were unable to miss the opportunity to cash in on such a well-known event, and some merchandise was produced and sold purely for profit. The Committee accepted that it was difficult to take action against these opportunists but urged the public only to buy items bearing the official Pie ‘88 logo, thus ensuring that the money would find it’s way back into the village and ‘not into an individual’s pocket’.

Goods from the day itself, such as napkins sponsored by Warburton’s, seasoning sponsored by Nestl¾, carrier bags sponsored by Naylor Bros. and sauce sponsored by Hammond’s, alongside dozens of other items, were kept by a mindful public knowing only too well the value of pie relics. The Souvenir Brochure, priced £1, and even the tickets for entry into the field were kept alongside other more dubious items. Temporary Bus Stop signs, bunting, police cones, public notices, ‘road closed’ signs and other more general signposts were collected by a voracious public, determined to possess something special to remind them of this unique Day.